RESEARCH IN THE REAL CLASSROOM

The Independent Investigation Method for Primary Students

RESEARCH IN THE REAL CLASSROOM is a series of grade-appropriate books based on the Independent Investigation Method, a seven-step research process that walks students through the fundamentals of research. Dedicated to showing teachers how to teach their students to conduct research, the Research in the Real Classroom series will also include companion books of teacher-developed units on popular themes and research strategies for each grade level.

The Independent Investigation Method for Primary Students
    Companion Books: Researching American Presidents
                                 Researching Intriguing Insects
                                 Researching Our Solar System
                                 Researching the Mystery of Magnets
                                 Researching Power of Plants
                                 Researching Tropical Rainforests
The Independent Investigation Method for Upper Elementary Students (planned)
The Independent Investigation Method for Middle School Students (planned)
The Independent Investigation Method for High School Students (planned)

RESEARCH IN THE REAL CLASSROOM

The Independent Investigation Method for Primary Students

CINDY NOTTAGE

VIRGINIA MORSE

Maupin House

MAUPIN HOUSE PUBLISHING, INC.
PO Box 90148
Gainesville, FL 32607

1-800-524-0634
352-373-5588
352-373-5546 (fax)

www.maupinhouse.com
info@maupinhouse.com

Publishing Professional Resources that Improve Classroom Performance

RESEARCH IN THE REAL CLASSROOM:
THE INDEPENDENT INVESTIGATION METHOD FOR PRIMARY STUDENTS

© 2003 Cindy Nottage and Virginia Morse
All Rights Reserved

COVER AND BOOK DESIGN: Gaye Dell

EDITOR: Mark Devish

ASSISTANT EDITOR: Lita Cunningham

Library of Congress Cataloging-in-Publication Data

Nottage, Cindy, 1943-
  The independent investigation method for primary students / Cindy Nottage, Virginia Morse.
    p. cm. -- (Research in the real classroom)
Includes bibliographical references and index.
  ISBN 0-929895-55-X (pbk.)
  1. Research--Study and teaching (Primary) 2. Interdisciplinary approach in education. 3. Education, Primary--Activity programs. I. Morse, Virginia. II. Title.
  LB1047.3.N68 2003
  372.139'43--dc21
                                    2003008027

DEDICATION

This book is dedicated to the hundreds of teachers who have proven that our youngest students can be researchers. Their creative units, ideas, and enthusiasm have been the inspiration for this book.

TABLE OF CONTENTS

INTRODUCTION

viii	Acknowledgements
ix	Notes from the Authors
x	About the Research in the Real Classroom Series
xi	About this Book

TEACHING EACH STEP

2	A "Prep" Step
	Laying the Groundwork:
10	Step 1: Topic
18	Step 2: Goal Setting
24	Step 3: Research
33	Step 4: Organizing
40	Step 5: Goal Evaluation
46	Step 6: Product
55	Step 7: Presentation

TEACHER RESOURCES

62	IIM Unit Plan Forms
74	Student Assessment Forms
90	Sample MLA Citations for Various Formats
92	References

APPENDIX

94	NCTE/IRA Standards for the English Language Arts
96	Definition of Terms Used in the Research Process
99	Reproducible Graphics

ACKNOWLEDGEMENTS

Special thanks to Karen West, who not only edited the rough draft of the manuscript but also kept media specialists at the forefront of this manual with her LMS Connections.

CINDY NOTTAGE   VIRGINIA MORSE

NOTES FROM THE AUTHORS

Our interest in developing a student-friendly research process began 18 years ago when we were teachers in an elementary-school enrichment program. We had planned a research assignment for our very capable students, and we were excited to get them started on the challenging but rewarding task of research. We had high hopes for the project, and felt that our students would be so interested in the assignment that they would tear into the library eager to begin learning on their own. However, instead of basking in the happy glow of a job well done, everyone ended up feeling frustrated and disappointed. We thought the students weren't trying very hard—they felt confused and helpless.

Just like you (who may have been disappointed by the results of your own carefully planned research project), we wanted our students to be successful and excited to do more. We did some research of our own, looking for materials to help us plan future assignments. Although we found isolated strategies, workbooks with activities, and lessons on how to write a research paper, nowhere could we find a complete process to support students in their assignments from beginning to end. So, we decided to create one ourselves.

Drawing on our many years of classroom teaching experience, we developed the Independent Investigation Method (IIM), the seven-step model on which this series is based. We couldn't believe how differently our students reacted during our second project: their attitudes towards research began to change as soon as we started to explain our step-by-step process. The idea that they were special detectives supported by a special process empowered them. Students who had been loudly opposed to the idea of research started begging to extend the scope of the assignment. When it was over, they wanted to know when they would get to do it again.

Nearly twenty years later, IIM (often said as "Double-I-M") has been used in thousands of classrooms world wide, with overwhelming success for both students and teachers. And now we travel all over the globe, conducting workshops and training sessions, and helping administrators and media specialists set up school-wide research programs. What fun! We get to meet so many talented people who are dealing with the same issues we encountered all those years ago. But now we get to offer real help—proven help—and to hear their success stories.

Now it's time for you to get started. We know you'll find the books in this series helpful, and a source for diminishing your frustration. Good luck! Let us hear from you as you work to help your students become special detectives called "researchers"!

RESEARCH IN THE REAL CLASSROOM: The Independent Investigation Method for Primary Students

Research in the Real Classroom shows you how to teach your students to do research. Each of the four sequenced core manuals is geared towards specific grade and skill levels, gives you a template to help you turn any curriculum unit that you already teach into a research unit, and each has developmentally appropriate lessons and examples to support you throughout the process.

About the Research in the Real Classroom Series (based on the *Independent Investigation Method*)

Because we think that school-wide implementation is the best way to teach students the importance of research as a life-long skill, we have designed each volume to be an integrated part of the series. However, each is freestanding—even if your middle school students have never been exposed to the process, the Middle School manual will show you how to give them the skills they need to become successful researchers.

The Research in the Real Classroom series is based on the Independent Investigation Method—IIM, the seven-step process that we developed 18 years ago. All children can become successful researchers using the IIM process—we know because we have seen students of all ages and abilities use it and learn that:

- Research is a sequential process used to answer questions.
- There are many sources for information.
- They must cite all sources using a standard bibliographic format.
- They must not plagiarize.
- Information must be analyzed, organized, and synthesized for use in a product.
- They should share their new knowledge with an appropriate audience.
- Enthusiasm and fun can be part of every research assignment.

We based IIM on findings which show that students must be specifically taught the process of research (Cassidy, 1989) beginning at a very early age and in a gradual, sequential, and cumulative way (Wray, 1988) that is integrated into the regular curriculum (Eisenberg and Brown, 1992).

- At the Primary Level (Grades K - 2), you work with your whole class researching one topic, and teaching your students the basic skills of research.
- The Upper Elementary Level (Grades 3 - 5) has your students apply those basic skills to work independently on individual topics.
- The Middle School Level (Grades 6 - 8) adds more difficult research skills to the students' knowledge base while keeping interest high for this challenging age group.
- Students at the High School Level (Grades 9 - 12) learn to integrate all their skills into in-depth, content-rich, authentic research projects.

Looking for ready-to-teach research units? To enhance each core manual, Maupin House has published companion theme books that combine the steps of our research process with topics that match your required curriculum: *Researching American Presidents*
Researching Intriguing Insects
Researching Our Solar System
Researching the Mystery of Magnets
Researching Power of Plants
Researching Tropical Rainforests

ABOUT THIS BOOK

RESEARCH IN THE REAL CLASSROOM: THE INDEPENDENT INVESTIGATION METHOD FOR PRIMARY STUDENTS

"Research for primary students?" you may be thinking. "Is that really possible?"

Glad you asked!

In the eighteen years that we've been training teachers to use IIM, we've found that not only is it possible to teach primary students a valid research process, it's imperative. In this high-tech age, all students need to master the component skills of research: critical thinking, the ability to gather, analyze, and synthesize information, and the preparing and presenting of products that share information with others. Students are never too young to learn these essential life-long skills.

It bears repeating that the Independent Investigation Method (IIM) is based on findings which show that students must be specifically taught the process of research (Cassidy, 1989) beginning at a very early age and in a gradual, sequential, and cumulative way (Wray, 1988) that is integrated into the regular curriculum (Eisenberg and Brown, 1992). This book—the Primary Level of the Research in the Real Classroom series—offers a comprehensive plan for integrating a school-wide research program into the curriculum you already teach. This process is successful for readers and non-readers alike. Each step of the process offers Novice, Advanced, and Teacher Tips that you can use to address your students' different levels of literacy.

THE PRIMARY LEVEL

OF THE INDEPENDENT INVESTIGATION METHOD (IIM)

Laying the Groundwork: A Prep Step

You will find that teaching the Seven Steps will go more smoothly by planning ahead, making connections for a powerful unit, and then introducing the process to your students.

Step 1: Topic

After introducing the class topic through immersion activities, you will work with your class to develop a graphic organizer that highlights what the students think they already know, and what they want to learn.

Step 2: Goal Setting

As a class, you and your students will formulate goal setting questions and identify additional research goals.

Step 3: Research

You will present the resources to your class, document each with the appropriate bibliographic heading, and record notefacts on chart paper as your students dictate them from each source.

Step 4: Organizing
Your students will work with you to organize their notefacts into categories.

Step 5: Goal Evaluation
As a class, you will check to see if your goals have been met.

Step 6: Product
With your guidance, your students will develop whole class, small group, or individual products that share the knowledge from the study.

Step 7: Presentation
Your students will present their product(s) to an appropriate audience.

Students will use these research skills in all their educational endeavors and beyond, so the earlier they are taught the research process, the better. Students need time to practice and internalize these sophisticated skills, and they will be more successful at the higher levels if they have a solid grounding in the process from the early stages.

RESEARCH IN THE REAL CLASSROOM
THE INDEPENDENT INVESTIGATION METHOD FOR PRIMARY STUDENT
will show you that:

- Research can be "hands-on" and understandable for even pre-K students.
- Primary students are capable of using advanced vocabulary and internalizing all the steps of a valid research process.
- Even non-readers can learn to view themselves as researchers.
- Reading and writing skills are advanced through the research process.
- When students are engaged in developmentally appropriate activities, they learn both the required content and the skills for their grade level.
- IIM is a cumulative, integrated approach that teaches young students a valid process that will not have to be abandoned for a "real" research process later on.
- By learning critical research skills at a very young age, students will be ready to become self-sufficient learners who will avoid plagiarism and develop into accurate, ethical, independent researchers.

At this level, we don't expect students to work independently. You will guide your whole class through the seven-step process using a topic that you choose from your existing curriculum—Native Americans, planets, rainforest, plants, or whatever you are expected to teach. We have provided the step-by-step directions, modifications for emerging as well as advanced readers, mini-lessons, samples, and reproducible pages that will make teaching the research process foolproof within your chosen unit. Non-readers and beginning readers can participate fully because you present information orally and visually, then record and display it on chart paper. You will see immediately how the required state and national standards for reading and writing (p. 94) are built right in.

"How will I find time for this?" you may ask.

Don't worry:

You will have enough time because you are going to teach the same curriculum that you have always taught, only in a new way. The skills you are teaching in reading and writing, the foundation of the primary curriculum, are the very ones that are applied and improved in the research process.

Similarly, materials should not be a problem.

Only three to four resources will be used for actual fact gathering, and your regular textbook can be one of them. Since this will be an adaptation of a unit you already teach, you can use the classroom supplies you have gathered over the years (with, of course, a few "must haves") to supplement your already chosen unit and teaching style.

You can follow our mini-lessons exactly, adapt them to fit your own classroom routine, use Ms. Kachina's lessons, or replace them with your own lessons. You have perfected many ways to teach, and we are not asking you to abandon them. Instead, we expect you to add your own flair when explaining our Key Skills to the very real children who walk through your door every day. Our mini-lessons are just meant to get you started. At the end of the study, the objectives built into the unit will be clearly observable in your students' ability to make and present a product that creatively shows what they have learned.

When you hear your kindergarteners ask, "When will we do our next research study?" or your second graders say "I'm ready to do my own study," you will agree that finally there is a method that takes the confusion and mystery out of the research process—both for teachers and for their young students.

PARTS OF THIS BOOK

THE STEPS OF THE PROCESS

Each step (from Groundwork Prep to Step 7) is set up to give you support as you teach your units the IIM way. The structure of each step enables you to complete the process using any curriculum unit—within that structure is flexibility that allows you to modify and enhance the process for your students' different levels of literacy using the many ideas in these chapters, as well as your own proven techniques.

Each step includes the following components:

INTRODUCTION
A short description of what will happen during the step introduces the process.

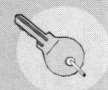

KEY SKILLS
We have chosen Key Skills based on the NCTE/IRA Standards for the English Language Arts (see p. 94) as the focus for each step of the process. These are boxed at the top of each step for easy identification.

TEACHER STEPS AND STUDENT STEPS
These are the specific instructions that you and your students will follow as you proceed through your chosen unit(s).

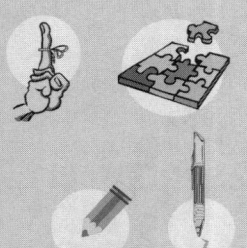

TEACHER TIPS AND LMS CONNECTIONS
We have included practical, helpful tips from the hundreds of teachers and library media specialists who have used the process and developed effective strategies for each step.

NOVICE AND ADVANCED
These strategies are included to give you other options when working with either very young/inexperienced researchers (Novice) or high ability/experienced researchers (Advanced). Choose from the different options at each step to modify the instruction for the grade and skill level of your students.

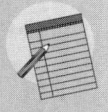

MINI-LESSONS
These classroom-tested mini-lessons give you the basics that will help you teach the Key Skills at each step. Use these lessons to get started. Later, you may want to supplement or replace them with your own tried and true lessons.

THE STEPS IN ACTION:
MS. KACHINA'S 1ST GRADE HOPI UNIT
Ms. Kachina, a fictional 1st grade teacher, takes her class through each step of the unit she has chosen (Hopi Native Americans). The summary of each step found in the complete unit plan Ms. Kachina has written is boxed at the top of each step for ready reference. You will see how she prepares for the unit and the many, different strategies she uses to carry out the plan she has created to empower her young students to do research. These strategies will give you different ideas from those in the mini-lessons.

FIGURES

Within each step, you will find a variety of figures to help you visualize what you are going to be doing and how your room will look.

This section contains a variety of resources to help you teach your students to be researchers.

TEACHER RESOURCES

IIM UNIT PLAN FORMS
These blank forms give you the structure to develop your own IIM curriculum units. The sample Hopi unit plan provides an example of how one teacher filled them out.

ASSESSMENT FORMS
These classroom-tested forms will help you assess both the process and end-products of your class's research study.

SAMPLE MLA CITATIONS FOR WRITING A BIBLIOGRAPHY
We have chosen the most commonly used resources and listed the format recommended by the Modern Language Association. A sample of each is included.

REFERENCES
These resources were used in developing this manual and have been helpful to us in teaching our students to be researchers.

REPRODUCIBLE GRAPHICS
These pages give you reproducible graphics to support the process and use on classroom charts and decorations.

APPENDIX

NCTE/IRA STANDARDS FOR THE ENGLISH LANGUAGE ARTS
The national language arts standards for grades K-12 are the foundation of this process and are reflected in the Key Skills for each step.

DEFINITION OF TERMS USED IN THE RESEARCH PROCESS
This list includes definitions and examples for terms used in this manual.

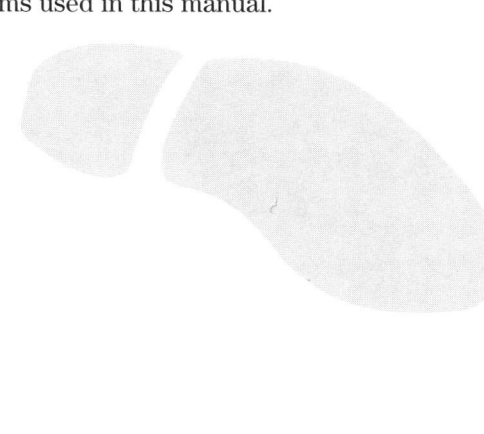

TEACHING EACH STEP

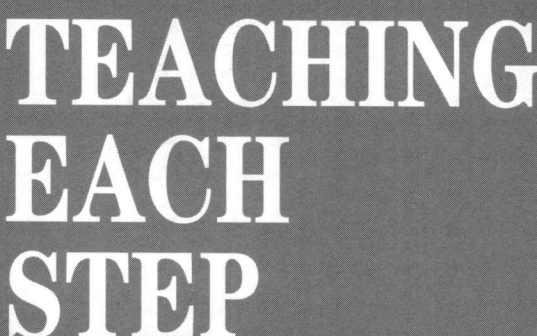

2   **A Prep Step:**
LAYING THE GROUNDWORK

10   **Step 1: Topic**

18   **Step 2: Goal Setting**

24   **Step 3: Research**

33   **Step 4: Organizing**

40   **Step 5: Goal Evaluation**

46   **Step 6: Product**

55   **Step 7: Presentation**

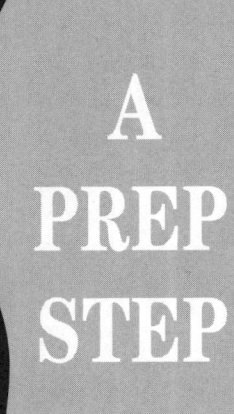

A PREP STEP

LAYING THE GROUNDWORK

You will find that teaching the Seven Steps of IIM will go more smoothly by planning ahead, making connections for a powerful unit, and introducing the process to your students.

Introduction

The Seven Steps of the IIM process have been designed to make it as easy as possible to convert one of your standard units into a research unit. However, there are some things you should prepare before you introduce the process to your students. You should start planning at least one week before beginning the unit.

The most important thing you will do is to pick a unit that is already part of your regular curriculum to teach in a research manner. Remember, you are choosing a topic that the whole class will be researching together. Choose one that you're familiar with, that you're required to teach, that you already have resources for, and that has defined learning outcomes that can be used to develop your standards-based Big Questions, which will be the foundation of your class's research. These are the major concepts you want your students to learn from studying this topic.

Once you've defined your Big Questions, you will need to decide how long you want to spend on your unit: three to four weeks of 30-45 minutes a day will give you plenty of time to introduce the process and teach the important content and research skills. You can use the blank unit plan forms to keep track of the different parts of your unit, and Ms. Kachina's completed forms as a guide for developing your own.

The remaining tasks—setting up the interest center, planning immersion activities, coordinating with other personnel, choosing resources for the research, and preparing materials and activities—will set the stage for a complete and exciting unit. Once these steps are completed, it will be time to introduce your students to the excitement of research using IIM.

KEY SKILLS

The student will
1. Understand the role of a researcher.

2. Be aware that there is a process for conducting research that consists of steps with specific outcomes.

TEACHER STEPS
You will

    a. Choose a unit of study from your grade-level curriculum to use as your research topic.

    b. Identify national, state, and/or local standards as the foundation of your unit.

    c. Contact your Library Media Specialist and invite him/her to collaborate with you.

    d. Build a unit plan. Be sure to include standards-based Big Questions that frame the study to keep it from being just a set of activities.

EXAMPLE:
State Standard: Understand that cultures must adapt to their environment in order to survive.
Big Question: Why was the Hopi tribe able to survive in its environment?

    e. Find three or four resources that will be used in Step 3: Research as sources of information. Each source should provide information related to the Big Questions. Don't limit yourself to non-fiction books–videos, interviews, or a trip to the museum are all valid resources. Including non-text sources will prepare your class to think beyond the encyclopedia and Internet, and will include students with different learning modalities.

RESEARCH IN THE REAL CLASSROOM: The Independent Investigation Method for Primary Students

f. Choose assessment strategies and tools that demonstrate that your unit objectives have been met (see Appendix, p. 62).

EXAMPLE:
Unit objective: Learn key vocabulary related to the study of the Hopi.
Assessment strategies: Play vocabulary game; complete IIM Glossary Chart (p. 15).

g. Set up your interest center with objects (books, magazines, pictures, artifacts, etc.) that are representative of your unit topic and that are displayed in a way that will raise the curiosity and interest of your students.

h. Plan immersion activities (field trip, speaker, video, story, etc.) that are designed to further student interest in the topic.

i. Coordinate with other teachers who may be involved in the unit (special ed, art, music, PE, etc.) and possible parent volunteers.

j. Notify parents about the unit and any presentation date(s), if applicable.

k. Put up a special bulletin board, with the title of the process (Independent Investigation Method), the IIM symbol, Agent IIM, and the names of the Seven Steps. Use one of your own design or purchase one (see p. 110).

l. Post your Big Questions either in the interest center or the on bulletin board.

m. Introduce your students to the research process by explaining IIM vocabulary, the logo, and the Seven Steps on your bulletin board (mini-lesson, p. 6).

n. Explain to your students that they will be special investigators called "researchers."

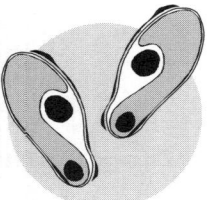

STUDENT STEPS
Your students will

a. Learn about the Seven Steps of IIM and the vocabulary and symbols associated with the process.

b. Understand that they will be special detectives called "researchers."

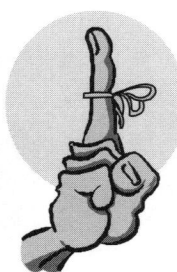

TEACHER TIPS

- The Unit Plan forms (p. 62) are included as a guide to identify key elements of the process and help you develop a plan to follow. If your existing curriculum units fit easily into this format, you may not want or need to use the forms.

- Grade levels can divide a unit into subtopics for each class within that grade level to research (for example, if your Kindergarten unit is plants, different classes might study trees, flowers, or vegetables). The presentation can then be one class "teaching" the other classes in that grade level about their subtopic.

RESEARCH IN THE REAL CLASSROOM: The Independent Investigation Method for Primary Students

- Throughout this manual, we have based the time needed for most mini-lessons on a 45-minute class period. You may want to break these sessions into smaller segments depending on the age and the attention span of your students.

- Spend extra time explaining the process if this is the first IIM unit for your students.

- If you have decided to use a unit that you've never taught before, be sure to do the background reading necessary for you to be well informed.

LMS CONNECTIONS

- Library Media Specialists (LMS) have a wealth of resources to share with classroom teachers.

- Many LMS also have experience in research skills and will enthusiastically support your project. Some even have the IIM bulletin board materials displayed in the Library/Media Center (LMC). When they are IIM-trained, they can use the same research vocabulary as you, which reinforces the work you are doing in your classroom.

- Many LMS will also reinforce the excitement and worth of your research project; students always love to hear that other adults are interested in their projects.

- The LMS may be willing to help with the immersion activities and choose literature related to your topic to read during any regularly scheduled media sessions.

- In some schools, the LMC has a display area for student projects and for mini-museum events. This may be important if there is not adequate space in your classroom.

NOVICE

- In writing your unit, be sure to include activities for your non-readers.

- The mini-lesson for this step works for all age researchers who aren't familiar with IIM. If your students have used IIM before, move on to Advanced.

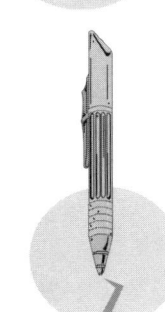

ADVANCED

- In writing your unit, be sure to add more challenging activities for your advanced readers.

- Do a quick review of the Seven Steps and have children talk about what they have done at the different steps. You could even do this as a writing activity or a game to see how many steps they can fill in.

MINI-LESSON
INTRODUCING STUDENTS TO THE IIM PROCESS

Curriculum Unit: _____ *(Your topic)*

Step: Groundwork

Time: 45 minutes

OBJECTIVES
Students will
- Understand the role of a researcher *(Key Skill 1)*.
- Be aware that IIM research is a seven-step process *(Key Skill 2)*.

MATERIALS
- IIM Bulletin Board
- Detective costume
- Large magnifying glass

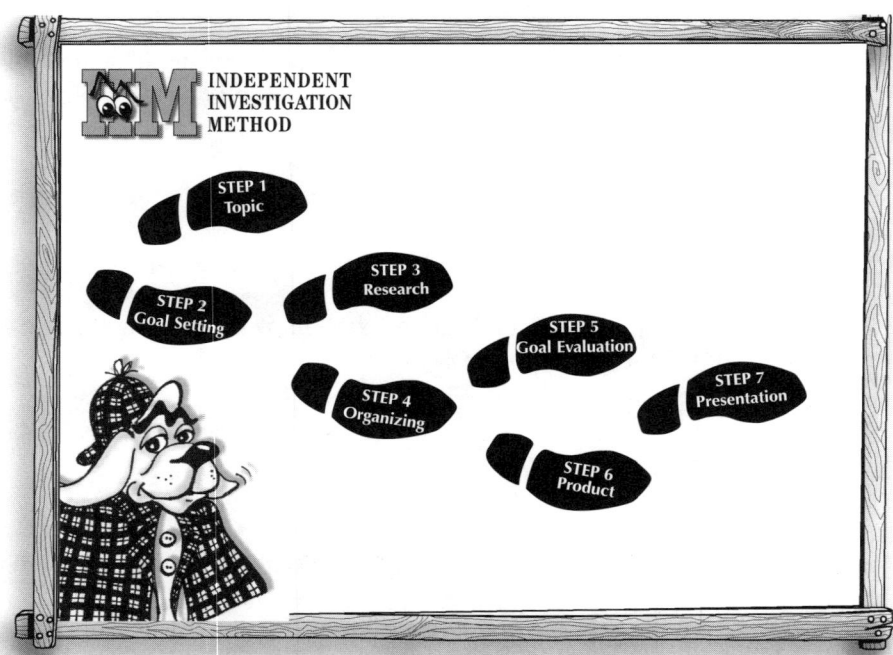

Figure 1:
IIM Bulletin Board

PROCEDURE

1. Explain to your students that the class is going to do research to find answers to the many questions about (fill in your class topic). Ask them what "research" is (finding new information about something of interest, looking for clues).

2. Point to the dog on the bulletin board as you introduce Agent IIM ("Double-I-M") as a special detective called a "researcher" who is there to help them.

3. Point to the IIM sign, ask them what "Double-I-M" stands for, and let them tell you what they think the meanings of the three words are:

INDEPENDENT -   *"Doing something by myself."*
INVESTIGATION - *"Looking everywhere for information."*
METHOD -   *"A plan to follow while looking for information."*

4. Have them locate the IIM symbol (the two eyeballs (II) and eyebrows (M) on the sign), and tell them that this symbol will remind them that they are special detectives called "researchers," who are looking everywhere for information.

5. Now show them the plan—the Seven Steps—and as you read the name and number of each step, ask them questions that allow them to relate each one to something in their own lives:

   STEP 1: **TOPIC**
   Our class topic is?
   What is something you'd like to know more about?

   STEP 2: **GOAL SETTING**
   What is something you'd like to be able to do in the future? What do you have to do to achieve your goal? In Step 2, researchers set goals for their study and work hard to achieve them.

   STEP 3: **RESEARCH**
   Where might we look to get information about our class topic? When something (like a book, video, or speaker) gives us information about our topic, we call it a resource.

   STEP 4: **ORGANIZING**
   How many of you have a messy desk, drawer, bedroom, locker? What happens when you want to find something? This Step is where researchers organize their information so they can understand what they have learned.

   STEP 5: **GOAL EVALUATION**
   What is the partner step for this? (Step 2: Goal Setting.) Now it's time to check to see if we accomplished the goals we set in Step 2 before we can go on.

   STEP 6: **PRODUCT**
   What's your favorite type of project? In this plan, we call those projects "products," and this is where we make or write something in order to share what we have learned. (Tell them what the product is if you've already made that decision.)

   STEP 7: **PRESENTATION**
   When you have learned something new, don't you like to share it? How do you feel if there's no one to tell about it? During our IIM unit, we will have learned many new things, and we will share the products we made in Step 6 with an audience. (Name the actual audience for their products if you have made that decision.)

6. Have them recite the names of the steps with you, and then tell them that it's time to get started.

NOTES

- You might want to dress up as a detective with a giant magnifying glass to introduce the process.

- If you make your own bulletin board set, be sure it contains a graphic of Agent IIM, the name of the process, the IIM symbol, and the step names and numbers.

LAYING THE GROUNDWORK: A Prep Step

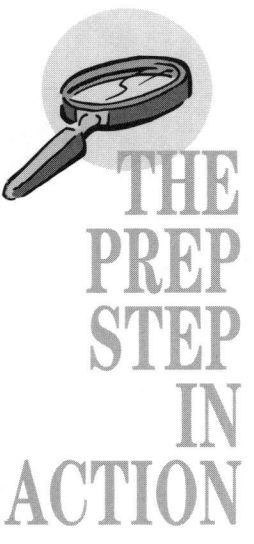

THE PREP STEP IN ACTION

GROUNDWORK PREP:
MS. KACHINA'S 1ST GRADE HOPI UNIT

- Plan unit. (See Teacher Resources section for complete Hopi Unit Plan.)
- Notify parents of upcoming unit and mini-museum day in class newsletter.
- Contact Silver Moon and Ms. Jones to schedule class visits.
- Meet with Mr. Bookworm, the LMS, to collaborate on resources, and on ways to reinforce the process and help advanced students.
- Meet with Ms. Ball, the physical education teacher, and Ms. Soprano, the music teacher, to discuss teaching Hoop dance and music.
- Meet with Mr. Brush, the art teacher, to plan lesson on making Kachina masks.
- Contact parent volunteers to oversee center activities and speaker's corner.
- Set up interest center.
- Introduce IIM by dressing as a detective.

LAYING THE GROUNDWORK

Ms. Kachina, a first-grade teacher, has decided to convert her unit on the Hopi Indians into a research unit. She has been teaching this unit for years, but this is the first time she has used IIM.

She is planning on integrating language arts skills with the social studies content inherent in the material. By integrating several subjects into the unit, she can spend more class time on the material every day. She has lots of resources that she can use for lessons, to fill her interest center, and to use as research sources. She begins to think of ways to make the unit as complete and exciting as possible. She meets with Mr. Bookworm, the Library Media Specialist, to see how he can work with her on this unit: what resources he has and ideas to help her top readers.

Ms. Kachina meets with the music, physical education, and art teachers to see if they can help her with lessons for the music, hoop dance, and mask-making activities that she plans on teaching. Coordinating with other teachers early in the year is a great way to build school-wide participation in a research program. She has arranged for parent volunteers to come in and help make sample products. She is excited to have Silver Moon, a native Hopi from the next town, come in to speak with the children. She meets with Silver Moon to discuss what background material the students should have before her visit. They schedule the best time for Silver Moon to present to the class.

Her IIM bulletin board is ready, with Agent IIM in Hopi garb, a map of the region they will be studying, and the Big Questions she has developed for the unit. She has chosen three resources that help answer her Big Questions to use as sources for Step 3: Research.

The interest center is growing because, in her weekly newsletter, she has alerted the parents to the up-coming unit as well as the mini-museum date, and many have been sending in items she can use. Ms. Jones has even offered to come in and show the children slides of her trip to the Hopi Mesas.

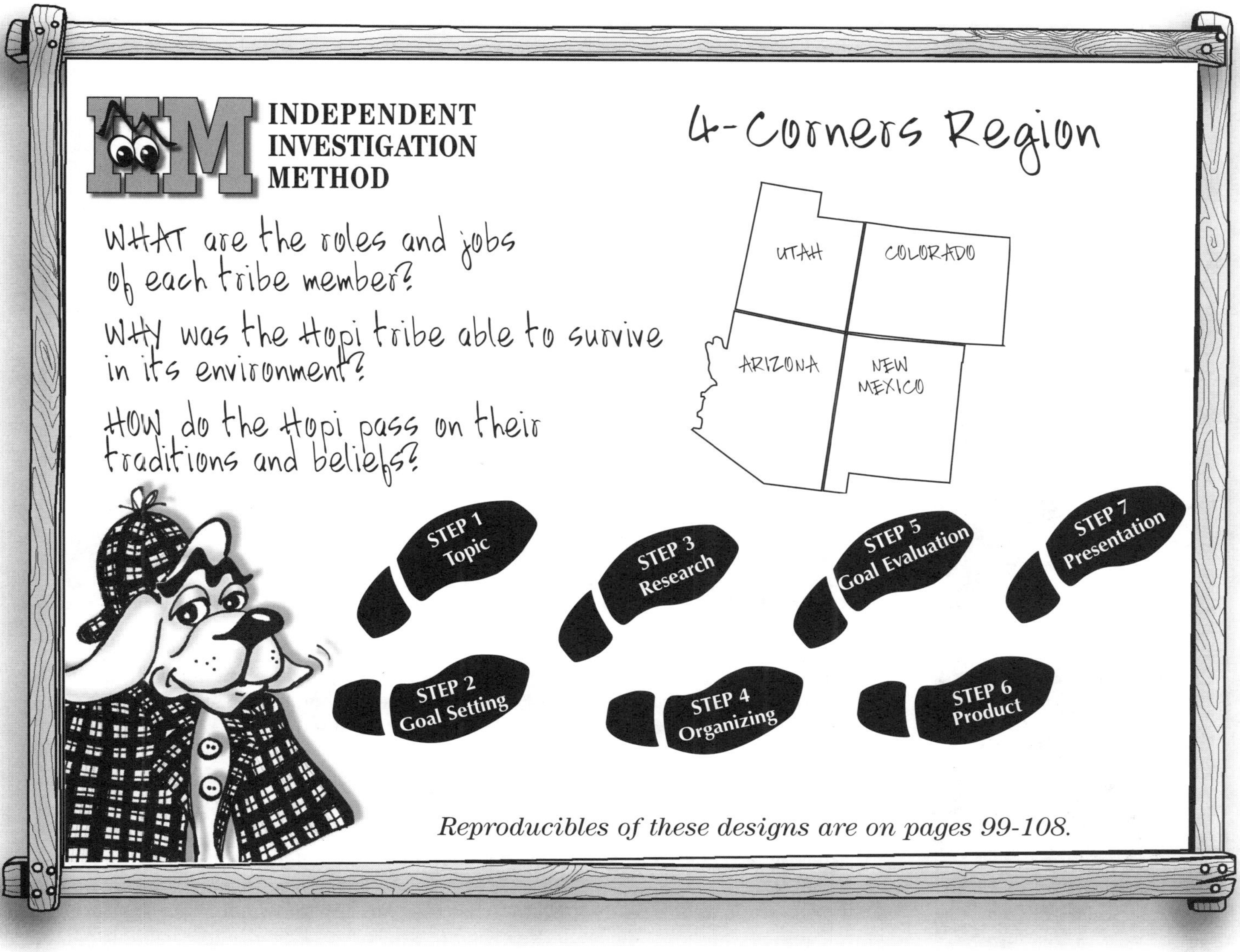

Figure 2:
IIM Bulletin Board in action

LAYING THE GROUNDWORK: A Prep Step

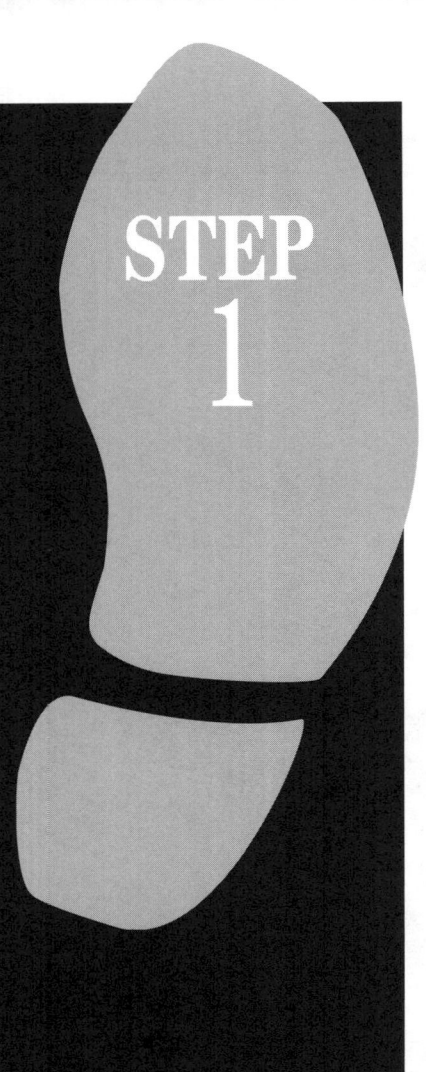

STEP 1

TOPIC

After introducing the class to the unit topic through immersion activities, you will work with your students to develop a graphic organizer on chart paper, focusing on what they think they know and what they want to learn.

Introduction

Now it's time to begin! You have already chosen the topic that you and your students will be researching together, and you have introduced them to the steps and concepts of IIM. Now they are ready to learn the skills they need to become researchers.

One of the best ways to introduce your students to the topic is by letting them explore your interest center. Reading to them, watching a video, taking a field trip, or listening to a speaker are also good immersion activities. The goal is to give your students enough information to pique their curiosity and generate excitement about the class topic.

Now your students are ready to share what they already know about the topic and to start thinking of other things that they want to know. These facts and questions can be listed on a graphic organizer, such as a concept map, a KWL chart, or any other form you choose.

The students also begin identifying important new words for their *Glossary* chart (mini-lesson, p. 15).

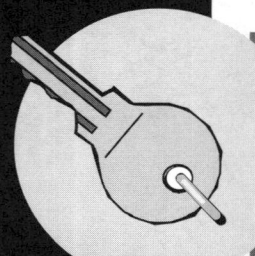

KEY SKILLS

The student will
1. Identify prior knowledge.

2. Formulate questions of interest about the topic.

3. Organize information on a graphic organizer.

4. Develop new vocabulary about the topic through listening and reading.

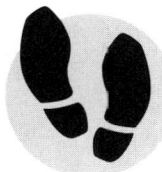

TEACHER STEPS
You will

a. Prepare a graphic organizer (such as a concept map—see mini-lesson, p. 13) and the *Glossary* chart (p. 15) using the graphics for the headings on pp. 102-105.

b. Explain to your students that they are on Step 1: Topic.

c. Immerse your students in the unit topic using a variety of means, such as your interest center, books, bulletin boards, posters, experiments, models, videos, speakers, and/or field trips.

d. Work with your class to complete the graphic organizer containing categories, prior knowledge, and questions.

e. Post and explain the *Glossary* chart, which will list important vocabulary words from the immersion activities and the graphic organizer.

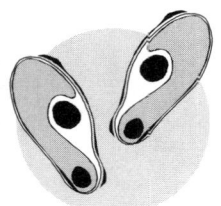

STUDENT STEPS
Your students will

a. Participate in the immersion activities that you choose, introducing them to the topic.

b. Contribute facts (what they think they know) and questions (what they want to know) to a graphic organizer such as a concept map.

c. Begin to identify new topic-specific words for the *Glossary* chart.

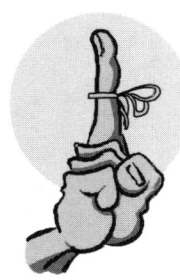

TEACHER TIPS

- Reinforce the process by saying the step number and name as you do each lesson.

- Immersion activities can take one or more days, depending on the depth of the initial knowledge you want your students to have before beginning their research.

- On the graphic organizer, accept all information students offer. Any misinformation can be used later as a learning tool.

- Spend extra time explaining the process if this is the first IIM unit for your students.

- When you have finished the formal lesson, you may want to allow students to add more details to the class graphic organizer with markers or paper strips until they begin Step 3: Research.

- The "K" section of a KWL chart can be used as the graphic organizer to record what students think they know.

- Instead of giving the graphics on your chart headings, you could handwrite and draw the Step numbers and names, and the IIM symbol ( ) explaining each as you put it on the chart.

STEP ONE: TOPIC

NOVICE

- If your students aren't readers/writers, send home one or two cutout shapes reflecting the topic (if your topic is Hopi Native Americans, your graphic might be a pueblo), and ask their parents to work with them to write a question and/or a fact on it.

- To help structure the lesson, you can pre-select categories to list on the concept map. (If your topic is plants, some sample categories might be "Care of," "Different Kinds," "Parts of a Plant," "What Plants Need to Grow.")

- You can write single words or draw pictures on the concept map for all the facts and questions as the children tell them to you.

- Work as a whole class, with you recording their ideas on the chart.

- Use pictures to help define the words on the *Glossary* chart.

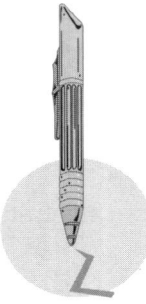

ADVANCED

- Have students complete individual concept maps on 8 ½" x 11" paper. Later, have them share their charts with the rest of the class. Their individual information can be added to the class's graphic organizer either by you or by them.

- Individual students can choose a sub-topic from the class unit topic to research independently (if your topic is plants, an individual's sub-topic might be orchids).

- Assign some students to be "Glossary Sleuths," responsible for finding the meanings of the new words.

- Have students keep their own word banks with the glossary words.

MINI-LESSON
ORGANIZING PRIOR KNOWLEDGE AND QUESTIONS ON A CONCEPT MAP

Curriculum Unit: _____ *(Your topic)*

Step 1: Topic

Time: 15 minutes

OBJECTIVES
Students will
Identify prior knowledge about the class topic *(Key Skill 1)*.
Formulate questions of interest about the topic *(Key Skill 2)*.
Organize information on a graphic organizer *(Key Skill 3)*.

MATERIALS
- A sheet of chart paper with "Step 1: Topic" written in the top left-hand corner, the IIM logo (eyeballs and eyebrows) drawn in the top right-hand corner, and a graphic design representative of your topic (for example, if your topic is Hopi Native Americans, you might choose a pueblo graphic to identify it) drawn in the center of the chart.
- One or two paper strips for each student
- Glue sticks and markers

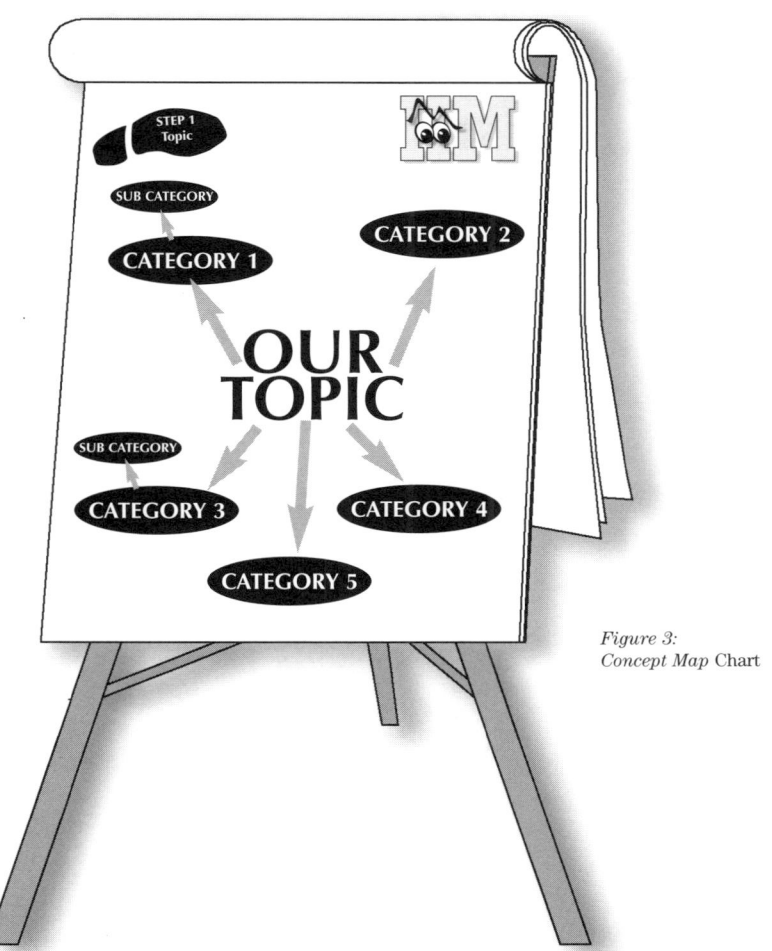

Figure 3:
Concept Map Chart

STEP ONE: TOPIC

PROCEDURE

1. Explain to your students that in Step 1: Topic, researchers first need to find out what they already know about the class topic. Once they identify that prior knowledge, they start asking questions about what they want to know.

2. Remind them that they already know something about the topic from the class immersion activities.

3. Give each student or pair of students one or two paper strips, and ask them to write either something that they already know or a question they might have about the class topic.

4. Show them the parts of the *Concept Map* chart.

    a. Step 1: Topic (Where we are in the process).

    b. The eyeball logo (We're looking inside ourselves for information).

    c. The graphic you've chosen to represent the topic. (This means that all the information on this chart will be about the topic.)

5. Have one student read what she has written on the strip and glue it to the chart.

6. Have another student do the same thing. As the students place their individual strips, they will need to decide whether to group it with other strips on the chart or put it in a new place. Be sure to have them explain their placements. After a few strips have been grouped together, have different students name the category. The goal here is to get your students to recognize groupings and categories. (As noted, if your students are novices, you might need to pre-list some categories.)

7. Continue with this process until all your students have placed their strips. Use different color markers to write category names as strips are grouped together.

NOTES

- Be sure there are both facts and questions on the chart. If you have time, have each child write one of each.

- Pairs work well if some students need help with the writing.

- You can use the graphics on pp. 99-108 to make your chart headings instead of writing/drawing them.

MINI-LESSON
FINDING NEW WORDS ABOUT THE TOPIC

Curriculum Unit: _____ *(Your topic)*

Step 1: Topic

Time: 15 minutes

OBJECTIVES
Students will
Develop new vocabulary about the topic through listening and reading *(Key Skill 4)*.

MATERIALS
- A sheet of chart paper with Step 1 and Step 3 footprints glued in the top left-hand corner, the IIM logo (eyeballs and eyebrows) glued in the top right-hand corner, and a title such as "Our (Your Topic) Glossary" written in the center.
- Markers

Figure 4:
Glossary Chart

PROCEDURE

1. Discuss the meaning of the word "glossary" (a list of words critical to the topic being studied).

2. Write your topic in the chart's heading.

3. Write one new glossary word (from the immersion activities) on the chart, and ask your students what it means.

4. When you agree on a meaning, write it next to the word.

STEP ONE: TOPIC

5. If no one knows, go back to the source or look in a dictionary. Be sure the meaning matches the way the word is used in connection with the class topic.

6. Explain that all good researchers record new, important words about their topic so when they've finished their study, they will sound like experts.

7. Ask them if they remember any other words from the immersion activities to put on the chart at this time

8. Continue adding words throughout the study.

NOTES:

- Explain the word "Glossary" by relating it to the terms you use for new, important words —Word Bank, Word Wall, Dictionary, etc.

- You can use "Words," "Word Bank," "Dictionary," or other terms for the title of this chart if "Glossary" seems too advanced for your students.

- Do this lesson during the same class period as your graphic organizer if you have time.

- Be sure the words are specific to the topic and aren't just new big words.

- Write the definitions or use pictures depending on the literacy level of your students.

STEP 1: TOPIC IN ACTION

STEP 1:
MS. KACHINA'S 1ST GRADE HOPI UNIT

- Make *Concept Map* and *Glossary* charts.
- Mr. Bookworm reads Hopi Legend to class.
- Show video of Hopi tribe as immersion activity.
- Identify location of Hopi on large map posted in interest center.
- Web information students know and questions they have about the Hopi on the *Concept Map* chart.
- Start *Glossary* chart with key words from immersion activities.

The interest center has been set up for a week. The children have had scheduled time to explore what is there.

RESEARCH IN THE REAL CLASSROOM: The Independent Investigation Method for Primary Students

During library time, Mr. Bookworm reads a Hopi legend to the class. Ms. Kachina tells them that they are ready to be the special detectives called "researchers." She reviews the Seven Steps of the IIM process with her students and reminds them what their topic is (Hopi Indians).

They watch part of a video about the Hopi, and Ms. Kachina leads a discussion about what they've seen. Now that her students have some ideas about their topic, Ms. Kachina has them look at the map on the bulletin board and shows them where the Hopi settlements are located in Arizona. They discuss direction words (north/south/east/west), and she has each child describe the Hopi's location from key landmarks on the map.

On the large *Concept Map* chart she has made (with a pueblo in the center), she has already listed some sample categories: location, housing, food, dress, jobs, and religion. Every child writes one thing (either a fact or a question) on a slip of paper, and Ms. Kachina asks for volunteers to read what they have written. Eventually, she has every student read their paper and place it on the *Concept Map*. She asks each student to explain why they have chosen the category in which they grouped their fact or question.

As a class, they start identifying important new Hopi words, and Ms. Kachina writes each one on the *Glossary* chart.

When each child has given at least one fact or question, and there are several new vocabulary words on the *Glossary* chart, it's time to end for the day. She tells them that they have been excellent researchers by completing Step 1: Topic.

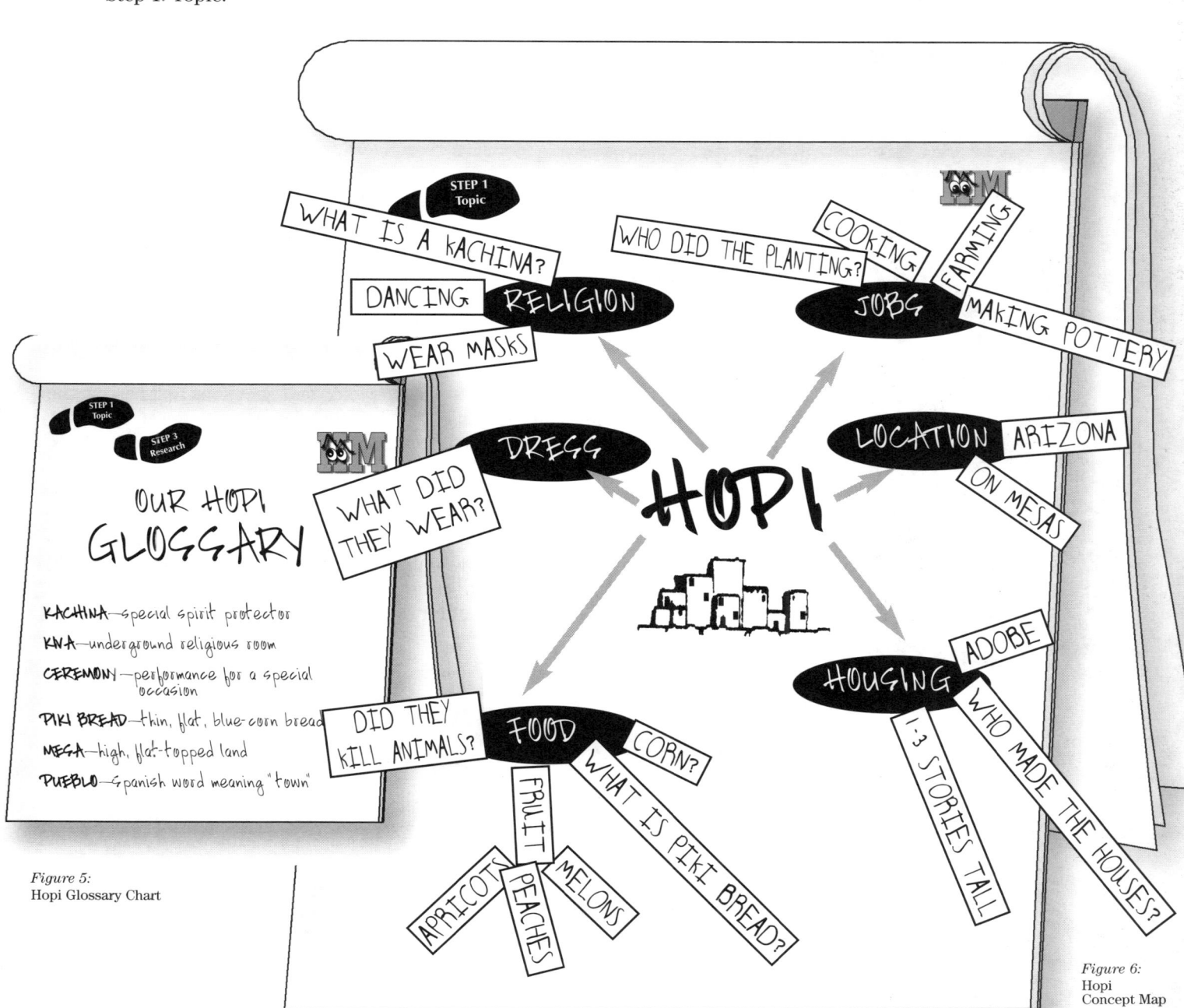

Figure 5:
Hopi Glossary Chart

Figure 6:
Hopi Concept Map

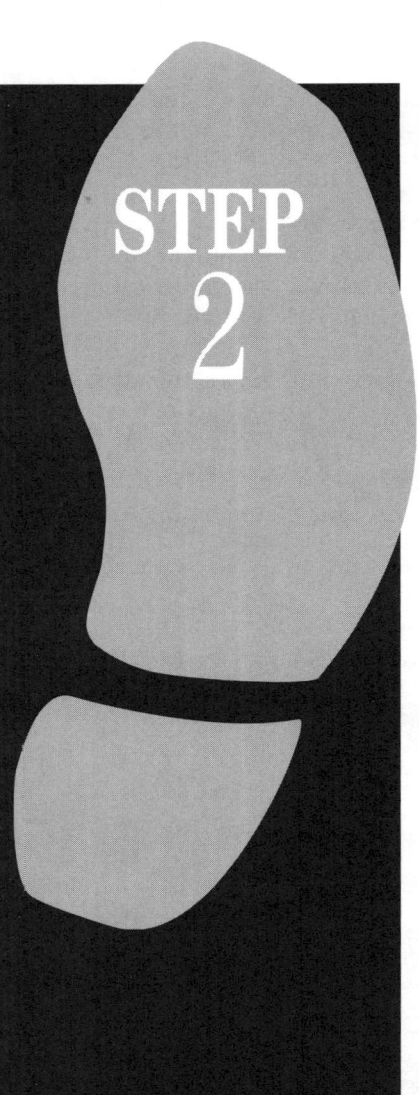

STEP 2

GOAL SETTING

You will work with your students to formulate goal-setting questions on a class chart and to identify additional research goals.

Introduction

As you move through your IIM unit, you can keep your students grounded in the process by quickly reviewing the steps with them, reminding them of what they have done and what they will be doing.

Step 2 is where researchers set important goals to help guide them in their study. Tell your students that researchers know what they are looking for before they start their investigation, so they will need to decide what it is they want to learn and how they will plan to get that information.

At the primary level, your students will mainly develop questions that narrow the topic into knowledge goals. There are many ways to help students develop good questions—use the ones that have been most successful for you. A good starting place is the graphic organizer your students created during Step 1.

Review the unit's Big Questions with the class, and let your students' curiosity help guide the discussion. When you honor their questions, they'll take ownership of the study. Your role as a master teacher is to dovetail what your students want to know with what you know they must learn. Help them develop sub-questions that narrow the topic in useful ways, so they can easily see what it is that they want to learn. In Step 3, their research will end up focusing on their four to eight most important sub-questions.

As students age and get more experience working with IIM, they'll have more complete control of Step 2. But with primary students, you'll need to identify the other goals that researchers set: how many sources of information will be used, how many notefacts you want them to find, and how many new words your class will need to add to the *Glossary* chart. These goals set the framework of the study and ensure that your students will fulfill the objectives you set for the unit.

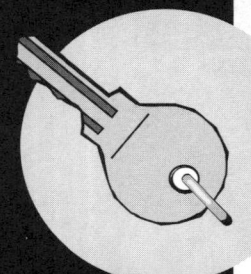

KEY SKILLS

The student will
1. Set concrete, measurable goals for the study.

2. Develop questions about the topic to direct the research.

3. Formulate different types of questions.

RESEARCH IN THE REAL CLASSROOM: The Independent Investigation Method for Primary Students

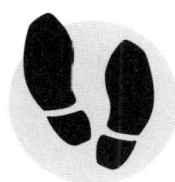

TEACHER STEPS
You will

a. Explain to your students that they are now on Step 2: Goal Setting.

b. Read the Big Questions you posted in your Interest Center or on your Bulletin Board to your class.

c. Help students formulate a variety of good questions related to or including the Big Questions, and list them on chart paper to be posted for the duration of the unit (mini-lesson, p. 21).

d. Explain that you have set additional goals for the study, and that your students will be required to find a certain number of resources, notefacts, and vocabulary words critical to the understanding of the topic.

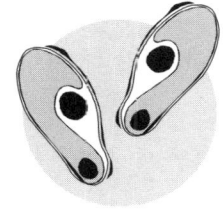

STUDENT STEPS
Your students will

a. Work as a whole class, in small groups, or in pairs to discuss/write good sub-questions related to the Big Questions.

b. Contribute questions to the class *Goal Setting* charts.

TEACHER TIPS

- You can make one class *Goal Setting* chart with a limited number of questions, or your students can work in pairs or small groups to formulate sub-questions for each Big Question.

- Your Big Questions should be broad, open-ended (floodlight) questions that will lead the class into research.

- Questions that focus on specific information (spotlight) are also important.

- Students' questions should include both floodlight and spotlight questions.

- If your students are working in groups, monitor them to be sure every child is participating in generating questions.

- Student-generated questions that are not chosen for the final *Goal Setting* chart can be sent home as a parent-child assignment.

- If you started with a *KWL* chart in Step 1, put the questions in the "W" column.

LMS CONNECTION

- The LMS can show students how to find information in an index using key words from the goal-setting questions.

STEP TWO: GOAL SETTING

NOVICE

- If posting the Big Questions would be too confusing for your students, just gather the questions your children give you and work with them to identify which would be the best to guide the study. If they miss some of your Big Questions, you can add them to the list.

- Introduce the question mark as punctuation.

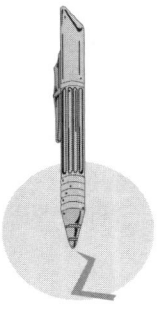

- If your students are having difficulty with the concept of "question," then review the different question-starting words (who, what, where, when, why, and how) and have them take one at a time to develop their list of questions for the study.

ADVANCED

- Give individual students copies of all the Big Questions and have them develop their own sub-questions.

- Write each Big Question on a different *Goal Setting* chart. Divide your class into the same number of groups as you have Big Questions and give one chart to each group. Have each group formulate and decide on three to six sub-questions and write them on their chart. Groups then present their Big Question and sub-questions to the class. These charts will be used as the class *Goal Setting* charts.

- Any sub-questions that are not chosen for the final *Goal Setting* chart can be used for independent research assignments.

MINI-LESSON
DEVELOPING CLASS GOALS FOR OUR STUDY

Curriculum Unit: _____ *(Your Topic)*

Step 1:   Goal Setting

Time: 45 minutes

OBJECTIVES
Students will
    Set concrete, measurable goals for the study *(Key Skill 1)*.
    Develop questions about the topic to direct their research *(Key Skill 2)*.
    Formulate different kinds of questions *(Key Skill 3)*.

MATERIALS

- One piece of chart paper for each of the unit's Big Questions, with "Step 2: Goal Setting" written in the top left-hand corner and the IIM logo (eyeballs and eyebrows) in the top right-hand corner. Write a Big Question as the heading of each chart. These are the *Goal Setting* charts.

- Pieces of lined paper with different Big Questions written as the title—one for each group of two to three students.

- Markers

PROCEDURE

1. Explain to your students that after finishing Step 1 by putting so much information about the topic on the class's graphic organizer, it's time to move on to Step 2: Goal Setting.

2. Ask them what it means to set goals. Encourage/accept a variety of answers that have to do with their personal lives.

3. Explain that researchers:
   a. Use Step 2 to set measurable goals for their study.
   b. Need to develop useful questions that they want to answer about their topic.

4. Discuss each Big Question. Tell your students that you want them to use the Big Questions as their starting points in order to develop further questions of study. Encourage their curiosity, and remind them how important it is that they develop questions in which they are really interested. Make sure they develop a variety of question types starting with different question words.

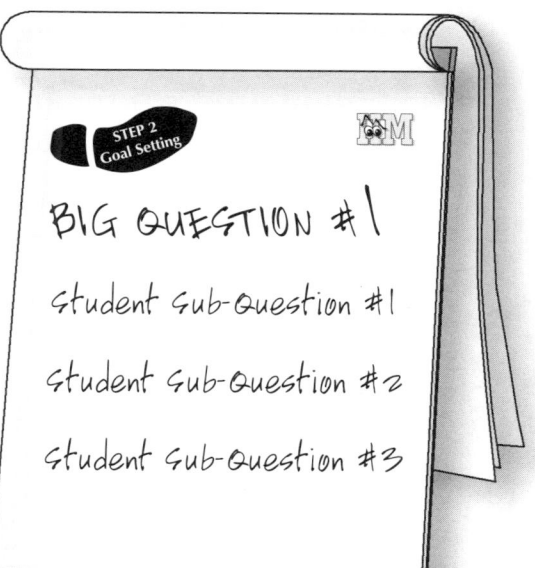

Figure 7: Goal Setting Chart

STEP TWO: GOAL SETTING

5. Start with one of the *Goal Setting* charts. Have your students find questions on the class's graphic organizer that relate to that Big Question. Write those questions on the chart.

6. Divide your students into groups of two or three. Give each group a paper with one of the Big Questions on it and have them discuss and write down as many sub-questions as they can in five minutes.

7. Have them reread their questions and decide on their two or three favorites.

8. For each *Goal Setting* chart, have the students who had that individual Big Question read and record their favorite sub-questions.

9. Work with the class to combine similar questions, and then choose three to four for each Big Question that will be used during the study.

10. Once the *Goal Setting* charts are complete, tell your students the other goals for their study:
    a. the number of resources they will use to find information.
    b. the number of notefacts they must find.
    c. the number of glossary words they will be required to add to their *Glossary* chart (set a realistic number for your grade level and topic).

NOTES

- When you're discussing resources for the study, you could make a list of where your students think they could find information about the topic. Star the ones you are going to use.
- Continue to remind your students that they are working as detectives.
- If your students are too young to work in groups and record their own information, do the lesson as a whole class.

STEP 2: GOAL SETTING IN ACTION

STEP 2: GOAL SETTING
MS. KACHINA'S 1ST GRADE HOPI UNIT

- Using question starters (who, what, where, when, why, and how), have students develop a list of questions about the Hopi related to our unit's Big Questions.
- Star six to eight questions that will be used along with the Big Questions to direct the class's research and write them on *Goal Setting* charts to be displayed throughout the unit.
- Identify additional goals: use three resources, find 35 notefacts, and learn at least eight glossary words.

RESEARCH IN THE REAL CLASSROOM: The Independent Investigation Method for Primary Students

Now it's time for the class to set goals for their study.

First Ms. Kachina reads the Big Questions on the Bulletin Board with her students. Next she shows them a chart entitled "Good Questions," with question-starting words listed on it. She has her students think of several questions for each starter, and she writes them on the board. When the students ask so many questions about food— *"Did they eat bear? Did they eat beans? Did they eat corn?"*—she helps them develop a broader question: *"What did they eat?"*

The class then decides which questions to use for their final *Goal Setting* charts. These are starred, and Ms. Kachina writes them on charts under the appropriate Big Question, and posts the charts to be used throughout the study.

She also lets the children know that there are other goals for this study. They will need to add eight new words to their *Glossary* chart, use three resources in Step 3: Research, and find 35 notefacts.

STEP 2 Goal Setting

What are the roles and jobs of each tribe member?
1. Did children work?
2. Who was the chief?
3. What did the medicine man do?
4. How did women help the tribe?

STEP 2 Goal Setting

How did the Hopi pass on their traditions and beliefs??
1. Why did they wear costumes?
2. Did they have story books?
3. What dances did they do?

STEP 2 Goal Setting

Why was the Hopi tribe able to survive in its environment?
1. What crops did they grow?
2. How did they build their houses?
3. What animals could they eat?

Figure 8:
Hopi Goal Setting charts

STEP TWO: GOAL SETTING

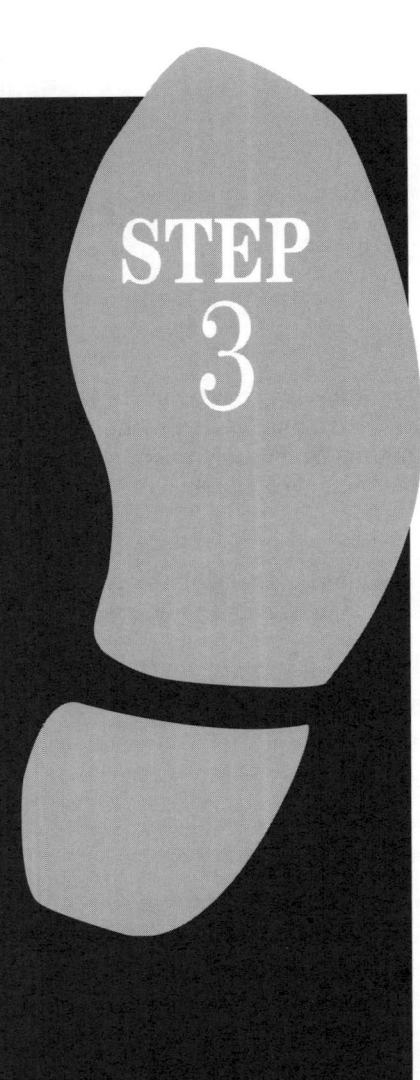

STEP 3

RESEARCH

You will present resources to your class, document each one with the appropriate bibliographic heading, and on chart paper record notefacts that your students dictate from each source.

Introduction

Finding, documenting, and recording facts is the essence of the research process. During Step 3, you will be helping your students develop good habits that will carry over when they begin conducting independent research studies either as extensions of your unit or in higher grades.

Your students are ready to look for new information. In Step 3, you model the lifetime skills of seeking and recording facts from valid sources. Plagiarism is explained, new vocabulary is identified, and paraphrasing is modeled and practiced.

At the Primary Level, you will be working with your students to gather information related to the questions developed in Step 2. Your first job will be to discuss what "plagiarism" is and how to avoid it (mini-lesson, p. 27). When your students understand that they cannot "steal" other people's ideas and words—that they must give credit for work that is not their own—it's time to learn the proper way to take notes.

You have already chosen three or four different resources that you will use as your sources of information. For the first source, reading a book passage to your students is the best beginning. It encourages accurate listening skills and prevents them from copying words from a text.

On the *Notefacts* chart (mini-lesson, p. 29), you will show them how to write a proper bibliographic entry for the first source. Identify it with "#1." Then read the appropriate passage(s) and gather notefacts from the source, recording them on the chart and marking each with "#1."

By varying the types of resources you choose, you will help your students understand that they can get information from many different places. Non-text sources (such as videos, posters, artifacts, field trips, pictures, and speakers) will expand their experiences beyond the encyclopedia and the Internet, and will include students with different learning modalities.

All your class's notefacts will be taken on charts and posted so you can review what has already been recorded before beginning each new resource. Once you've recorded the information from your three to four sources and added your words to the *Glossary* chart, you've completed Step 3 and are ready to begin organizing your information.

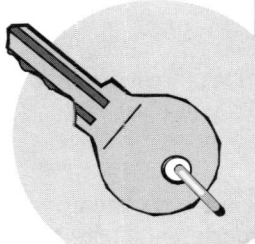

KEY SKILLS

The student will
1. Use a variety of appropriate text and non-text resources for the class topic.

2. Document each source in correct bibliographic format.

3. Gather detailed information based on goal-setting questions by listening, observing, and/or reading.

4. Formulate notefacts by paraphrasing and summarizing.

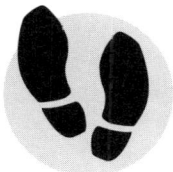

TEACHER STEPS
You will

a. Prepare *Notefacts* charts for each resource.

b. Explain to your students that they are now on Step 3: Research.

c. Teach the concept of "plagiarism" (mini-lesson, p. 27).

d. Introduce the first class resource (Source #1), write the appropriate bibliographic information on the *Notefacts* chart, and put "#1" in the magnifying glass (mini-lesson, p. 29).

e. Have your students focus on the goal-setting questions as you read from the resource.

f. Model paraphrasing from the passage and how to write short, meaningful notefacts.

g. As you record your class's notefacts, demonstrate that notefacts are
- Short phrases, not sentences.
- Learned from that source.
- Written in your students' own words.
- Complete enough to make sense.
- Related to the goal-setting questions.

h. Put "#1" in the magnifying glass that you've drawn next to each notefact.

i. You can use a piece of chart paper with no heading for overflow notefacts since the number in the magnifying glass will identify the source.

j. Add new words to the *Glossary* chart.

k. Repeat steps c-i with each source, giving each its own number (#2, #3, #4, etc.).

l. Post all completed *Notefacts* charts in your classroom.

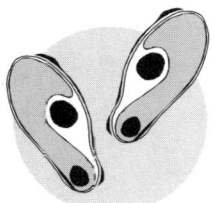

STUDENT STEPS
Your students will

a. Dictate notefacts from each source for you to record on *Notefacts* chart paper.

b. Identify and learn key glossary words.

STEP THREE: RESEARCH

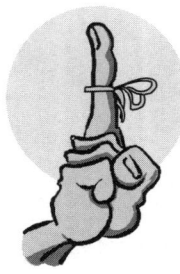

TEACHER TIPS

- Even though students may read individually about the topic, they will not be researching independently. They will be working as a whole class with the resources you choose and present.

- Vary the types of resources you use with them. It's fun to get information from watching a video or TV program together, having you read to them, conducting experiments, listening to a speaker, etc.

- You can use sentence strips for notefacts and organize them in a chart holder.

- Shorten notefacts by leaving out articles, adjectives, verbs, etc. This will help students personalize the facts with their own words when they use them in a written product.

- Taking notefacts from pictures in texts or posters is a good activity that encourages focused observation skills.

- If you started with a KWL chart, you can write notefacts in the "L" column.

LMS CONNECTION

- Library media specialists can prepare a list of additional sources for the teacher.

- The LMS can model notefact-taking as she reads literature (both fiction and non-fiction) that is related to the unit.

NOVICE

- Shorten the bibliographic citation to include only the essential information.

- Notefacts for very young students can be pictures or just one word.

- For a text source, read the whole selection (not too long) to your class first. Then, reread a short passage for note taking. Continue the same way with the rest of the selection.

ADVANCED

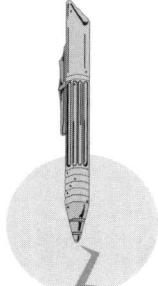

- Your independent readers can read a selection on the topic and report to the class as "experts." This information may become another *Notefacts* chart.

- Have the class read a common selection and highlight key words. Make a transparency of the selection, and let students highlight on the overhead. Then have them turn that information into notefacts that you record on the class chart. Carefully monitor their notefacts for plagiarism as you write them on the chart.

- Have a small group research a sub-topic (for example, if your unit is the Hopi, a sub-topic might be Ceremonies) and make their own product to share with the class.

- A small group can use an additional resource and record both bibliographic information and notefacts on chart paper to add to the class's notefacts.

MINI-LESSON
NO MORE PLAGIARISM!

Curriculum Unit: _____ (Your Topic)

Step 3: Research

Time: 10 minutes

OBJECTIVES
Students will
  Document each source in correct bibliographic form *(Key Skill 2)*.

MATERIALS
- Anti-Plagiarism chart or poster
- *Notefacts* charts

PROCEDURE

1. Write the word "plagiarism" on the board or point to it on your plagiarism poster, and tell your students that Agent IIM says, *"Don't be a Plagiarist."*

Figure 9:
Anti-Plagiarism Poster

2. Explain that a plagiarist is someone who steals other peoples' words or ideas.

3. Ask them how many have written books or drawn pictures they are proud of. Discuss what it would feel like if someone copied their words or took one of their pictures and pretended it was his/her own work.

4. Point to the word "plagiarism" again and tell them that's what plagiarism is—stealing.

5. Explain that since, as researchers, they will be learning from work that others have done, they must give credit to the person who wrote the words or created the ideas by stating where they got their information.

6. Show them the *Notefacts* chart heading and explain that it gives credit for each different resource the class uses by listing the author's name and the resource title. Introduce the term "bibliography."

7. Point to the big magnifying glass and explain that the word "source" refers to the specific resource they are getting their information from and that each source they use will get a number.

8. Have them understand that by writing a bibliography, they are being honest, not careless and lazy.

NOTES

- Keep the word "plagiarism" posted in the room. You can make your own poster or purchase the *IIM Plagiarism Poster* (p. 111).

- Very young children can understand the concept of plagiarism as long as you relate it to their own lives.

- This lesson is the introduction to the mini-lesson on page 29. If you don't use them together, you might want to write the bibliographic information on the *Notefacts* chart for Source #1 during this lesson.

MINI-LESSON
WRITING AND DOCUMENTING NOTEFACTS FROM DIFFERENT SOURCES

Curriculum Unit: _____ *(Your Topic)*

Step 3: Research

Time: 30-40 minutes

OBJECTIVES
Students will

Use a variety of appropriate text and non-text resources for the class topic *(Key Skill 1)*.
Document each source in correct bibliographic format *(Key Skill 2)*.
Gather detailed information based on goal setting questions by listening, observing, and/or reading *(Key Skill 3)*.
Formulate notefacts by paraphrasing and summarizing *(Key Skill 4)*.

MATERIALS
- Your first information source
- A *Notefacts* chart
- Markers

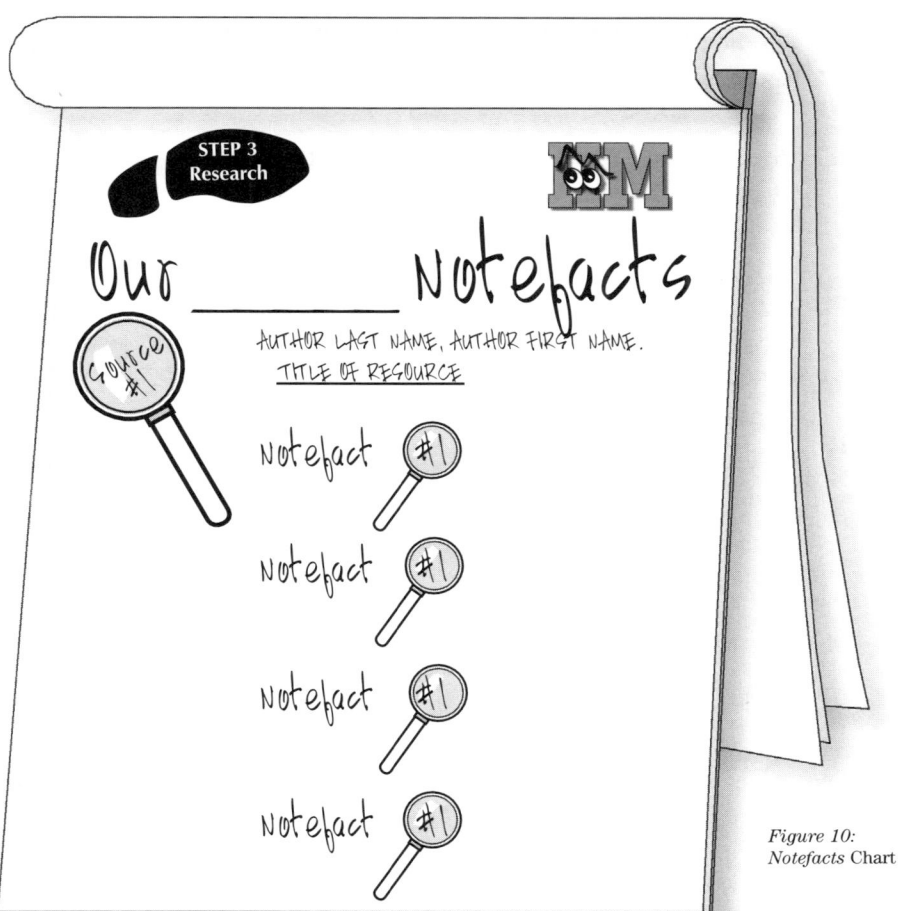

Figure 10:
Notefacts Chart

PROCEDURE

1. Tell your students that:
   a. They are now ready to find new information related to their goal setting questions.
   b. Researchers record answers to their goal setting questions as notefacts:
      Note: a short written piece like a thank you note to Grandma.
      Fact: something we know to be true.

2. Practice taking someone else's words and rephrasing them as notefacts in an activity like this one:

   Write this sentence on a piece of chart paper: Christopher Columbus sailed across the blue Atlantic Ocean and was the first person to find America.

   Read it to your class and say to your students: *I'm going to help you make those words into a notefact. First let's get rid of words we don't need.*

   Cross out words until it looks like this: "Christopher Columbus sailed across Atlantic Ocean—first to find America."

   Great! Now we've taken out words we don't need so it is short. Let's change some words so they are our own. There are at least two words we must have in our notefact. What are they? (Columbus and America) Now let's add the details in our own words. "Columbus crossed Atlantic—discovered America." That's excellent. You now have a notefact that is short and true but contains enough information so we can understand it.

   Practice this with other sentences if necessary. If your students understand the concept, go right to your Source #1.

3. Tell them it's time to begin research on their topic. Give them the title and author of their first resource, and tell them it will be referred to as "Source #1".

4. Write the author's name (last name first), the book title (underlined), and put a #1 in the magnifying glass showing this is Source #1, using a simplified but accurate format. (See p. 90 for the complete MLA bibliographic format for the most commonly used resources.)

5. Read a passage to them and start recording their notefacts, reminding them of the previous lesson. Remember to put a "#1" in the magnifying glass you draw next to each notefact to show it's from Source #1.

6. Have them look at the *Goal Setting* charts to focus their research.

7. Use a new sheet of chart paper for overflow notefacts. Just be sure to identify which source number it comes from.

NOTES

- Review Teacher Steps e-j as a guide for taking notefacts.

- Reading a book or book passage as your first source allows you to go back to the selection if your students give inaccurate information or can't remember details.

- At this level, use only the essential bibliographic information (see p. 90 for the complete MLA format). Add the details as your students become more proficient.

- Continue to work with your students, modifying each notefact so it's short and isn't taken verbatim from the text.

- Find new words from this source and add them to the *Glossary* chart.

- If your students need more work creating notefacts, practice paraphrasing in assignments for other subjects.

- Use the same notetaking procedure with each source you use for research.

STEP 3: RESEARCH IN ACTION

STEP 3: RESEARCH
MS. KACHINA'S 1ST GRADE HOPI UNIT

- Prepare three *Notefacts* charts.

- Define plagiarism and notefact for students.

- Show *The Hopi*, and identify title and author.

- Write proper bibliographic information on *Notefacts* chart and "#1" in the magnifying glass to identify it as Source #1.

- Read the class a passage from the book, having them think of facts that relate to the goal-setting questions.

- Record notefacts on chart, putting a #1 in magnifying glass next to each notefact

- Post *Notefacts* chart next to goal-setting questions.

- Do same steps with Source #2—*Native Americans of the Southwest* (video), and Source #3—speaker Silver Moon.

- Continue to add words to the *Glossary* chart.

- Mr. Bookworm works with top reading group to gather additional notefacts from fourth source.

STEP THREE: RESEARCH

The children are excited to get going on their research.

Ms. Kachina asks them where they think they should look for answers to their goal-setting questions. She writes all their ideas on a chart: books, magazines, Internet, computer programs, a trip to Arizona, museum, artifacts, posters, videos, library, a Hopi tribe member, e-mail. Wow! They are all impressed with the many places they could look.

Ms. Kachina tells them that for this study, they will use a book, a video, and a visit from a tribe member, Silver Moon. She then talks to them about plagiarism and introduces Source #1.

The students start dictating notefacts, and their collection begins to grow. During the week, they get information from all three sources and add more words to the *Glossary* chart. Her three top readers go to the library to work with Mr. Bookworm in writing additional notefacts from a fourth source that they will add to the class notefacts.

The walls are decorated with the charts the class is putting together. There is information about the Hopi everywhere. Ms. Kachina tells her students how impressed she is. They are becoming real researchers, and it shows.

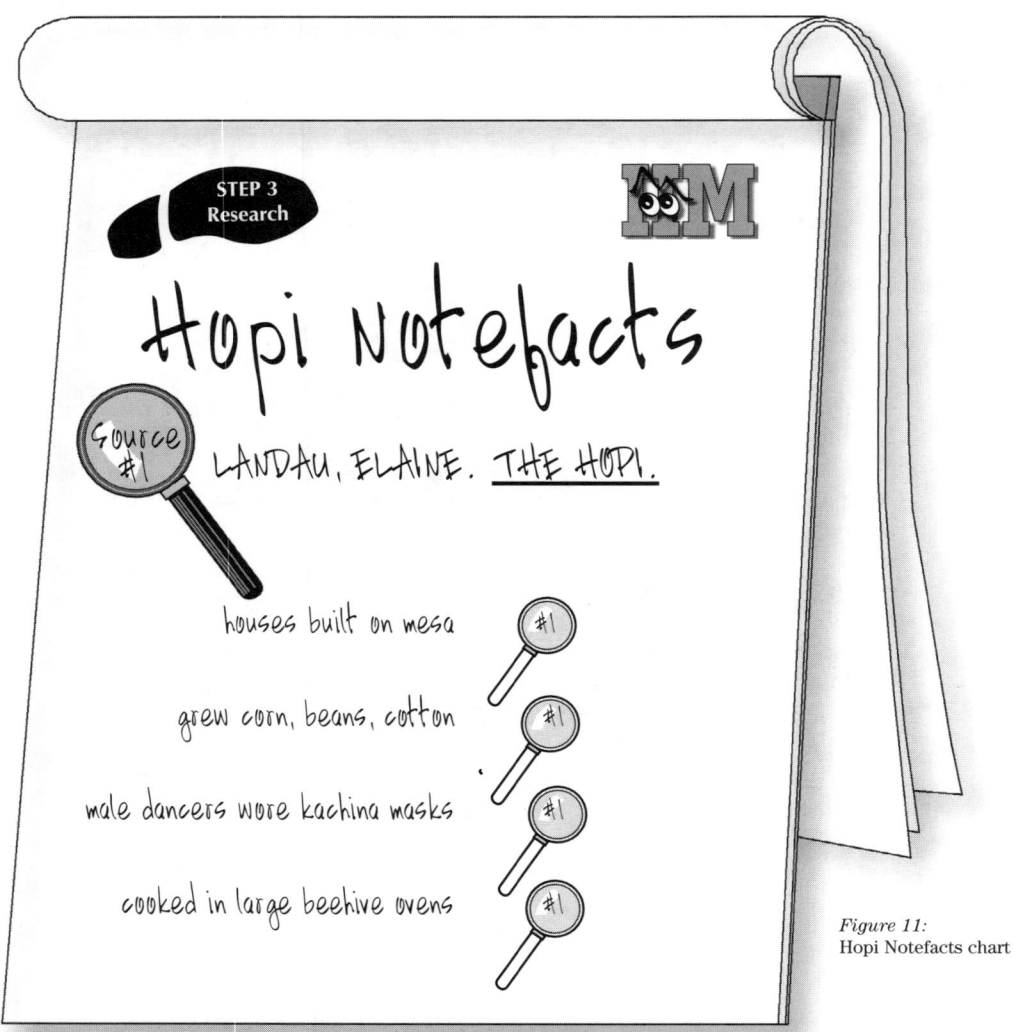

Figure 11:
Hopi Notefacts chart

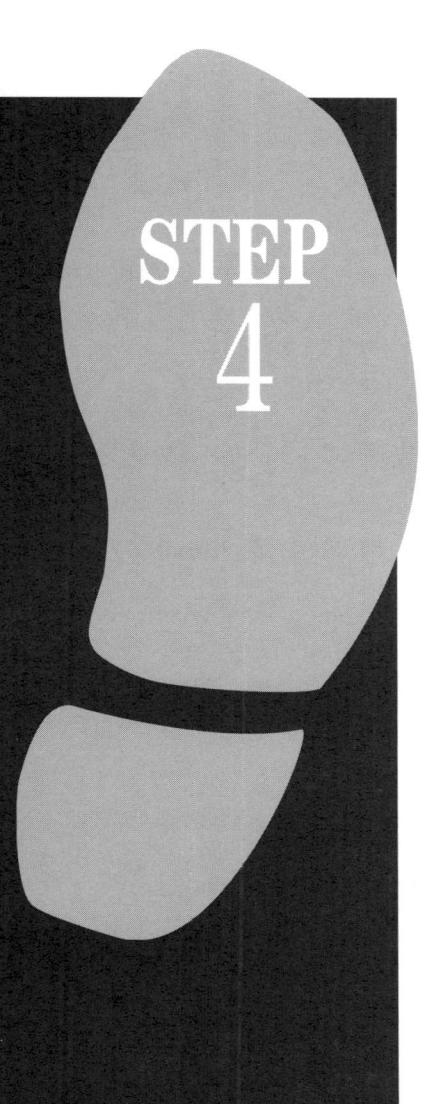

ORGANIZING

You will work with your students to organize all notefacts into categories on chart paper.

Introduction

All the gathering of information is done. Your *Notefacts* charts are hanging on the walls. There's an impressive list of new vocabulary words on your *Glossary* chart. Now it's time to analyze your information and regroup it into categories so it will be easier to use when making products.

To make sorting and organizing your research as easy as possible, you will actually cut individual notefacts from the *Notefacts* charts and then reassemble them on new, categorized charts. You can choose the categories yourself, or help your students form them through reviews and discussions of Step 1's graphic organizer, the unit's Big Questions, the class's goal-setting questions, and/or new connections they have made while gathering information. As your students organize the notefacts, they practice valuable critical-thinking skills while justifying their placements on the *Organizing Notefacts* charts.

This is an exciting time for your students. The research they have done becomes their own as they analyze and synthesize it in understandable ways. As the information becomes personally important to them, the way to effective products is paved.

When the *Organizing Notefacts* charts are completed, it's time to use that information to review the initial goals of the study and plan for the sharing of what your students have learned.

KEY SKILLS

The student will
1. Summarize and organize information from multiple sources.

2. Organize information in systematic ways by listing in categories.

STEP FOUR: ORGANIZING

TEACHER STEPS
You will

a. Prepare *Organizing Notefacts* charts for several categories.

b. Explain to your students that they are now on Step 4: Organizing.

c. Reread notefacts with your students, looking for categories. Step 1's graphic organizer and Step 2's goal-setting questions may be used for ideas (mini-lesson, p. 21).

d. Write category names on *Organizing Notefacts* charts and assign a different color for each one by coloring in the magnifying glass handle.

e. Cut the *Notefacts* charts into strips. Save the bibliographic headings to post later.

f. Model category choice with several notefacts. Choose some examples that will fit into more than one category, and explain your reasons for your final category choice.

g. Color in the handle of the magnifying glass on each notefact to match the category chosen, and glue the notefacts on the appropriate chart.

h. Give one notefact to each pair of students once they understand the process.

i. Have them choose a category for their notefact and explain the category choice to their classmates.

j. Have them color the handle of the magnifying glass to match their category choice and glue the notefact on the chart.

k. Continue until all pairs of students have explained and placed their notefacts.

l. Let pairs place additional notefacts without explaining their category choice to the class until all notefacts are placed.

m. Post all *Organizing Notefacts* charts and *Notefacts* chart headings (to reinforce the importance of the bibliographic information) for use in Steps 5-7.

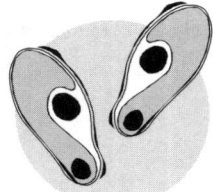

STUDENT STEPS
Your students will

a. Choose names and colors for their categories.

b. Choose categories for individual notefacts.

c. Defend their category choices.

d. Color the handle of the magnifying glass on each notefact to match the chosen category.

e. Glue notefacts on the appropriate *Organizing Notefacts* charts.

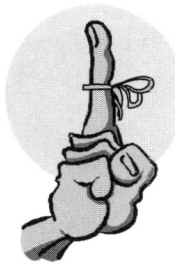

TEACHER TIPS

- To shorten this step to one lesson, do steps a - d yourself and start by showing your students the categories you have chosen. Begin your lesson with step e.

- Although the class's graphic organizer and goal-setting questions may be used for category ideas, don't be limited by them. Exciting critical thinking takes place when new connections emerge.

- If available, use different colored butcher paper for each category. Students would color in the notefact magnifying glass handle to match the paper color.

- A legitimate category should have at least three notefacts in it. If the class considers a "slim" category to be important, you could go back to one of the sources you already used and get some more notefacts for that category.

- A "miscellaneous" or "other" category is possible but should have no more than three notefacts in it.

- Use the *Organizing Notefacts* charts for a class lesson in developing topic sentences.

- If you have used a KWL chart, you can organize the information by color-coding the questions in "W" and coloring the facts in "L" to match the questions.

LMS CONNECTION

- The LMS can help find additional sources for categories that have slim information.

- The LMS can expand an area of miscellaneous information in which a student has shown strong interest so it can become an additional category.

NOVICE

- If your students are non-readers, place all the notefacts into categories as a class.

- You may want to pre-name categories for students or glue several notefacts with commonalties on each *Organizing Notefacts* chart. Work with the students to name the categories.

- Pair non-readers with readers for this step.

- Give students one notefact to expand into a complete sentence, with enriched language and details.

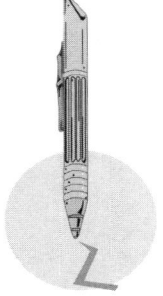

ADVANCED

- Once the notefacts are sorted into categories, have students work in small groups or individually to develop topic sentences for the categories and then write a paragraph using the notefacts.

- Students can make an outline from the *Organizing Notefacts* charts.

- Give small groups of competent readers another resource and a blank *Notefacts* chart. Have them write notefacts from that source for categories that need more information.

MINI-LESSON
NAMING CATEGORIES

Curriculum Unit: _____ *(Your Topic)*

Step 4: Organizing

Time: 30 minutes

OBJECTIVES
Students will
Summarize and organize information from multiple sources *(Key Skill 1)*.
Organize information in systematic ways by listing in categories *(Key Skill 2)*.

MATERIALS
- Product containers (cereal, soup, dairy, snacks, drinks, etc.)
- Posted *Notefacts* charts

Figure 12:
Organizing Notefacts Chart

PROCEDURE

1. Count—with your class—the total number of notefacts they have gathered about the topic.

2. Explain that good researchers use Step 4: Organizing to put their notefacts in some kind of order so they will be more usable.

3. Tell them that they will do that by rearranging the notefacts into categories.

4. If they're unfamiliar with the concept of categories, show them the product containers you have gathered and have them identify the sections and shelves in a grocery store where each would be found.

5. Next, read all the notefacts to them and have them think of possible categories. The graphic organizer from Step 1 and the *Goal Setting* charts from Step 2 are good places to begin.

6. Write their ideas on the board or chart paper.

7. Explain that these are good possibilities, and that you will think about them that evening and choose some for the class to use.

8. After class, choose the categories, set up the *Organizing Notefacts* charts, and cut up the original *Notefacts* charts.

9. The next day, complete Teacher Steps f - m.

NOTES

- If your students need more practice, play other category games during the day to reinforce the concept.

- It's easier for them to understand the concept of categories when you connect it to something familiar to them—colors of clothing, hair, eyes, etc.

STEP FOUR: ORGANIZING

STEP 4: ORGANIZING IN ACTION

STEP 4: ORGANIZING
MS. KACHINA'S 1ST GRADE HOPI UNIT

- Prepare *Organizing Notefacts* charts with web categories on colored butcher paper.
- Read all notefacts with students, making sure they are complete and understandable
- Have parent volunteers cut notefacts into strips.
- Model placement of notefacts on charts using several strips that can fit into different categories.
- Color handle of magnifying glass to match category choice, and glue notefact on chart.
- Give remaining facts to pairs of students, making sure there is a reader in each pair.
- Have students make decisions about category placement, explain choice and reasons to classmates, color magnifying glass handle, and glue notefact to chart.

The walls are covered with an impressive array of Notefacts *and* Glossary *charts.*

Ms. Kachina has recorded 35 class notefacts and 12 glossary words. Before starting Step 4, she has reviewed the notefacts and decided that the categories the class used on Step 1's graphic organizer will work for the organizing.

She prepares a different colored chart for each category: blue=location, green=housing, red=food, orange=dress, purple=jobs, and yellow=religion. She sets up an "Organizing" station with colored markers and glue sticks.

When the class begins, she has the children read the notefacts from each chart, making sure each child gets to read one. When all the notefacts have been checked to be sure they make sense and are complete, the parent volunteers begin to cut the notefacts into strips. While they are doing that, Ms. Kachina shows the students the *Organizing Notefacts* charts and uses three notefacts to model the organizing procedure. She points out that the notefact "corn—very important" could go either under "Religion" or "Food" and that they must choose which category to place it in. She models the placement of two more notefact strips, and then her students are ready to work independently.

Ms. Kachina sets the timer for three minutes, and allows pairs of students to discuss category placement for one notefact. Parent volunteers walk around the room to give help with reading if necessary. When the timer goes off, each pair has a turn to read the notefact to the class, explain where it will be placed, and go to the "Organizing" station to color and paste. Two pairs of students can't agree on the category, so the class listens to their reasons and then votes. Ms. Kachina gives the remaining notefacts out to be placed in categories without an explanation and is available to help if necessary. She evaluates their work on the IIM Teacher Observation Checklist (p. 75).

The parents are so impressed with the reading and critical thinking skills the children display. They are a real help when the pairs get stuck and need a little support.

When the notefacts are all in place, it's time to move to the next step, where the students will look back at the process to see if they've really achieved the goals they set in Step 2. They will also start planning how they will share their new information.

Figure 13:
Hopi Organizing Notefacts charts

STEP FOUR: ORGANIZING

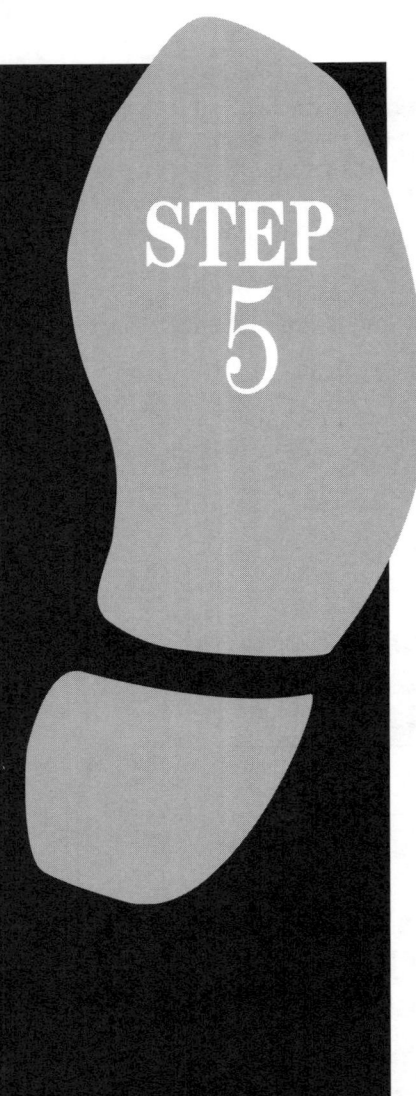

GOAL EVALUATION

You and your students will check to see if the goals set in Step 2 were met.

Introduction

Now that their information has been neatly arranged, your class can really see that they have learned a lot about the topic. They're getting anxious to start developing creative ways to share their new-found facts. But before they do, it's important that they review the goals set in Step 2.

Explain to your students that Step 5 is where researchers make sure they haven't missed anything. If they need to, they can gather additional information before they begin working on their products.

Have they used the required number of resources? Have they found and learned enough glossary words? Have they found information about the unit's Big Questions? What about the class's goal-setting questions? Only when you're sure that those goals have been accomplished can you move on to Product and Presentation.

You can do this step informally in class discussions or have your students complete activities—either individually or in groups—that will give you the information you need to assess their new learning. Use the methods you feel the most comfortable with. We have included some useful assessment forms in the Teacher Resource section of this book (p. 61).

KEY SKILLS

The student will
1. Retell specific details and draw conclusions from information gathered.
2. Use compiled information and knowledge to check on original goals, raise additional questions, and tell about experiences.

TEACHER STEPS
You will

a. Explain to your students that they are now on Step 5: Goal Evaluation.

b. Check knowledge acquisition by having your class give answers to goal-setting questions, either orally or in writing (mini-lesson, p. 43).

c. Review the other goals set in Step 2 (number of glossary words, sources, notefacts, and resource types) to see if they were achieved.

d. Use other ways of evaluating that are appropriate for your grade level and the topic: spelling/vocabulary tests, small group discussions, individual conferences, fact games, etc.

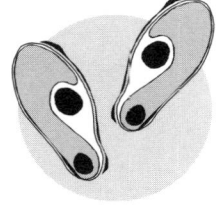

STUDENT STEPS
Your students will

a. Gather around the initial *Goal Setting* chart(s) and give information about those questions.

b. Find additional notefacts, if necessary, to answer the original questions.

c. Complete other assigned evaluative activities.

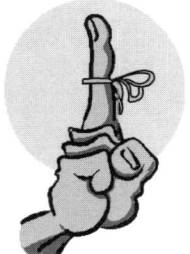

TEACHER TIPS

- Students need to understand that Step 5: Goal Evaluation is the step of the process where researchers look back at what they've done and take time to do more work, if necessary, before sharing their findings.

- Be sure that what you evaluate matches your unit plan's objectives. For example:

    OBJECTIVE: *Children will know the meaning of key vocabulary words pertaining to the topic* (Glossary chart).

    EVALUATION: *Students will label a diagram using correct scientific terms.*

- If important goal-setting questions have not been answered during the research, you might use an additional resource or find more information in a source you've already used.

- Some goal-setting questions may not be answerable. Understanding this becomes part of the learning process.

- This is the time to add more notefacts and/or glossary words if those goals were not met.

- Picture dictionaries, tri-folds with three facts and illustrations, and illustrated fact cards are visual ways of seeing what students have learned.

- A timeline of facts focusing on ordinals (first, second, third, etc.) helps students with sequencing skills if the facts relate to time order.

- Some goal-evaluation activities might take more than one class period to complete.

- This is a good place to record any new questions the students have that could be used for further research studies or for independent work.

STEP FIVE: GOAL EVALUATION

LMS CONNECTION

- Again, the LMS can help an excited student find additional information about research questions important to him/her.

- The LMS can create an activity to see if the students understand how to find information in books (index, table of contents, glossary) and/or can locate where the different types of resources they used in this study are found in the media center.

- Any evaluative information the LMS has observed during the research process will be important to the classroom teacher.

NOVICE

- Students can draw a picture illustrating a fact and explain it to the class.

- As a circle activity, let students choose one fact to expand into a more complete explanation.

- Pair non-readers with readers for this step.

- Make memory cards with glossary words on one side and pictures on the other. Play as a whole class or in small group to check for vocabulary development.

- Have each child choose one word to write and illustrate for a class big book picture dictionary.

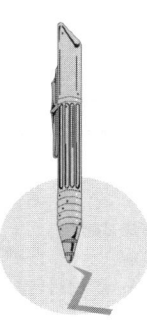

ADVANCED

- If some goal-setting questions weren't answered, have individual students do independent research to find answers.

- Students with good language-arts skills could develop a class topic dictionary.

- Have students write summary paragraphs using key glossary words to extend their writing skills.

MINI-LESSON
WHAT DID WE LEARN?

Curriculum Unit: ———————————— *(Your Topic)*

Step 5: Goal Evaluation

Time: 45 minutes

OBJECTIVES
Students will
Retell specific details and draw conclusions from information gathered *(Key Skill 1)*. Use compiled information and knowledge to raise additional questions and tell about experiences *(Key Skill 2)*.

MATERIALS
- *Goal Setting* chart(s)
- *Organizing Notefacts* charts
- A pointer

PROCEDURE

1. Explain to your students that Step 5 is where researchers make sure they have learned what they wanted to at the beginning of the process.

2. Ask them where they set the goals for the study *(Step 2: Goal Setting)*.

3. Review the goal-setting questions with them.

4. Point to the *Organizing Notefacts* charts and explain that these show how much they have learned about those questions.

5. Read each goal-setting question individually with at least one fact that they have learned.

6. If they have difficulty answering, point to a category where there is pertinent information.

7. Explain that if some questions weren't answered, the class can use one of the sources from Step 3 to find that information.

8. See if this research study has raised any new questions, and write them on a blank chart.

Figure 14:
Goal Setting Questions Chart

STEP FIVE: GOAL EVALUATION

NOTES

- Be sure every student gives at least one response to a question.
- Allow your students to give facts that may not have been written but were learned during the unit.
- If there were other goals set in Step 2: Goal Setting, be sure to check those as well.
- Let your students use the pointer to identify a question and give an answer related to it.
- The new questions can be used for independent research studies.

STEP 5: GOAL EVALUATION IN ACTION

STEP 5: GOAL EVALUATION
MS. KACHINA'S 1ST GRADE HOPI UNIT

- Conduct an oral check to see if students have used three resources, found 35 notefacts, identified eight glossary words, and found answers to the goal-setting questions.
- Play a vocabulary game to review glossary words.
- Have students fill out My Words at Work (p. 76) and make three picture and vocabulary cards illustrating and describing glossary words.
- Have students mark location of Hopi on an outline map of 4-Corners region and write at least one sentence describing where the tribe is located.

It's been such fun finding all the notefacts and putting them into categories.

Now Ms. Kachina can't wait for her evaluation to show that her researchers have really learned something.

First, she reviews the goals set in Step 2, checking to make sure her class met all their goals and found all their information. Did we use three resources? Yes, we did. Did we find more than eight glossary words? Yes, we found 12. Did we write at least 35 notefacts? Yes, we wrote 45. Did we find answers to our goal-setting questions? Ms. Kachina thinks her students have, but she isn't sure. She goes through the list of questions, has each child give one fact to answer it, and evaluates their work on the IIM Observation Checklist (p. 75). They really did get the information they were looking for!

Ms. Kachina has made 15 different "Hopi" grid cards with all new glossary words in different squares. Pairs of students play using candy corn for markers. Ms. Kachina reads the definitions of the words, and the children put markers on the space where the word is found. The winners call out "Hopi" when they fill in a line and get to eat their candy corn.

Next each student chooses three words, fills out My Words at Work, (p. 76) and makes sets of picture and word cards for each word on the sheet. Now they can play memory games with their friends. Ms. Kachina is sure that all the children are competent with the new vocabulary words.

Finally, she gives each child an outline map of the 4-Corners region and has them mark where the Hopi live and write a sentence describing the location using direction words. This goes well, but Ms. Kachina notes that they need a lot more work with direction words.

She is satisfied that her students have learned much—now it's time for them to share that information with their parents.

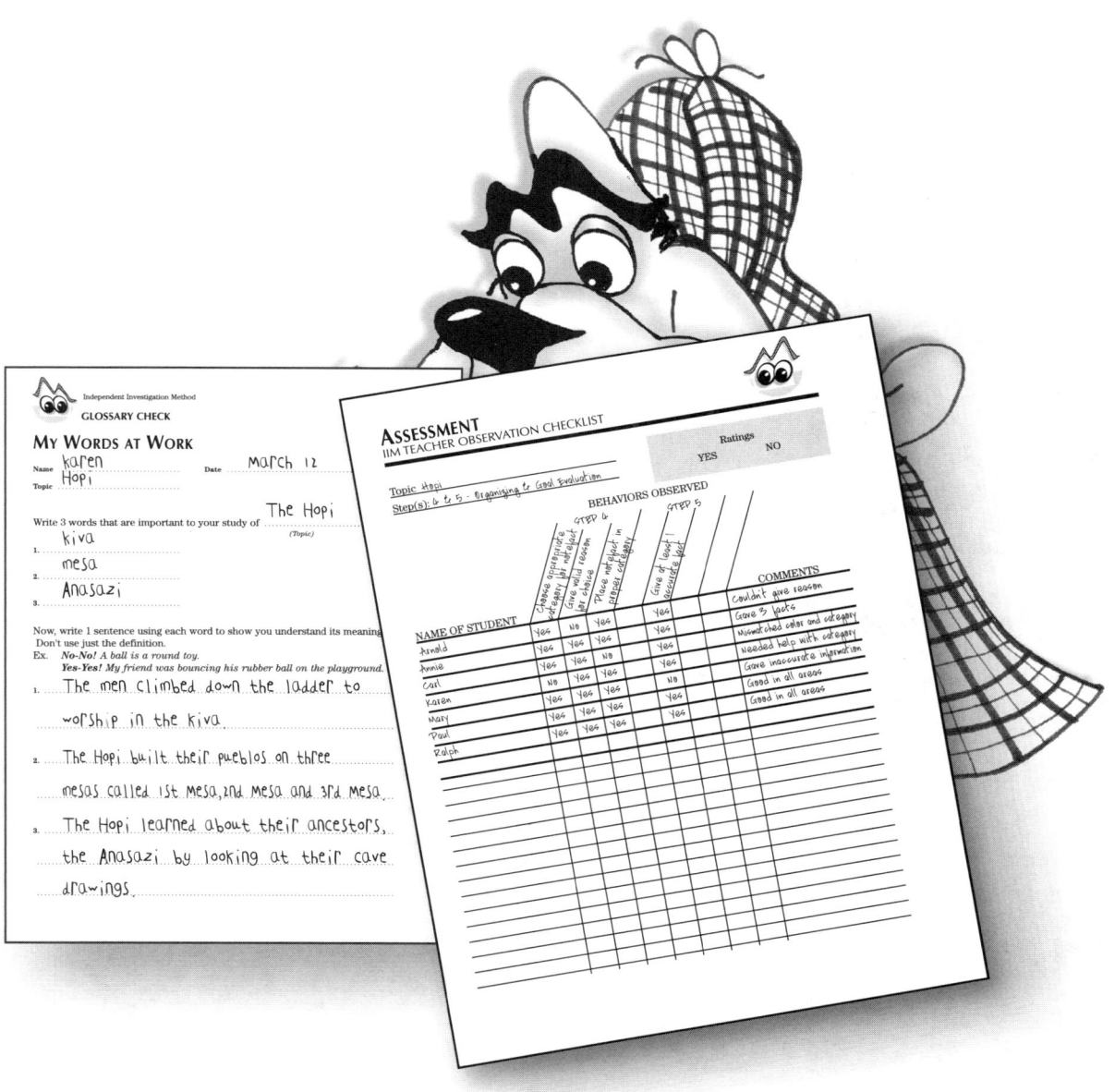

Figure 15:
Ms. Kachina's Assessment Forms

STEP FIVE: GOAL EVALUATION

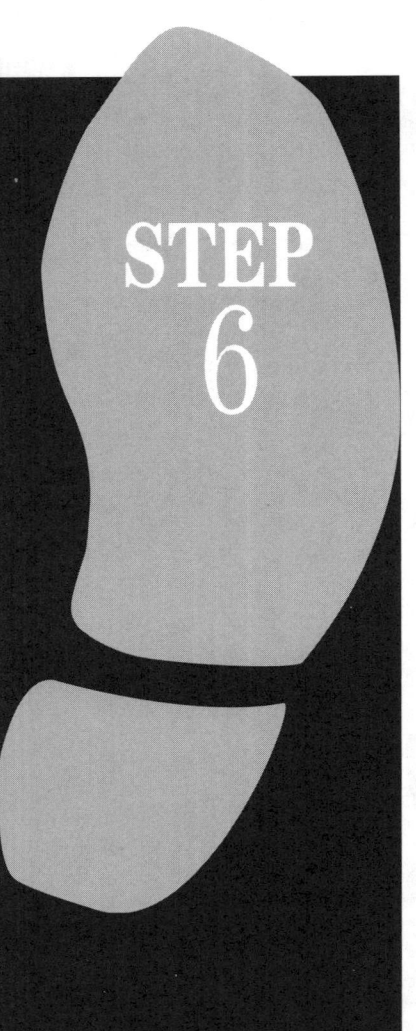

STEP 6

PRODUCT

Your students will share their new knowledge by developing whole class, small group, or individual products based on quality standards.

Introduction

Products can take many forms. You can choose to have your students complete a group project (such as a play, a mural, or a class book), have all the students work individually on the same type of product (posters, models, games, or fact books), or let each child choose from a list of products (p. 54). No matter how you decide to assign products, remember that the purpose is for your students to let others know what they have learned during the research study.

Writing can be a part of every product, but it doesn't have to be in report form. Poetry, narratives, acrostics, letters, and plays let your students experience the joy of using writing in its many creative ways. There are also many products that don't require writing. Murals, posters, maps, dance, crafts, and models help children share information in non-verbal ways.

Encourage creativity in your classroom: even if everyone is working on the same type of product, stress how important it is for all students to express their individual uniqueness. Researchers need to show what they've learned in their own varied ways.

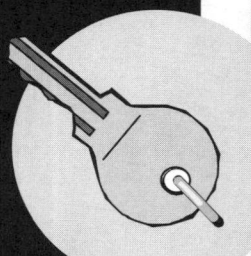

KEY SKILLS

The student will
1. Represent information in a variety of ways.

2. Select, organize, and produce visuals to complement and enhance meaning.

3. Produce final, edited documents and projects.

RESEARCH IN THE REAL CLASSROOM: The Independent Investigation Method for Primary Students

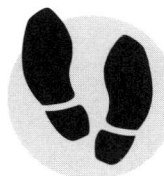

TEACHER STEPS
You will

a. Explain to your students that they are now on Step 6: Product.

b. Decide the best way (group or individual products) for your class to share the knowledge they have gained from the research unit. Books, plays, bulletin boards, posters, songs, murals, dances, reenactments, graphs, and timelines are all effective choices. (See p. 54 for a list of additional ideas.)

c. Work with your students to develop a rubric or checklist for making the quality product you have chosen (mini-lesson, p. 49).

d. Teach the important skills for making a quality product.

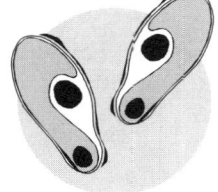

STUDENT STEPS
Your students will

a. Work with you to identify components of a quality product.

b. Practice the important skills that will help them make a quality product.

c. Create a class, small group, or individual product based on the *Quality Product* checklist.

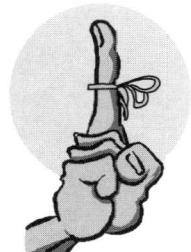

TEACHER TIPS

- Choose a product that matches your topic, audience, and class skills.

- Teach your students the skills necessary for developing a specific type of product. For example, with posters you may need to teach lettering, measuring, and the use of space for graphics.

- If the product is a report or includes a written component, model using the *Organizing Notefacts* charts as the basis for paragraph development.

- Assigning all students to develop their own version of the same product type still allows them to display differences in knowledge acquisition, ability level, and learning style.

- For cooperatively produced products, you can give a group grade or grade each child's part individually.

- If the students are working on a cooperatively produced product, be sure that they know exactly what their role is. For example, if the product is a mural, an individual's responsibility might be background, trees, animals, or houses.

- If students are making individual products, remind them to get key information from the *Organizing Notefacts* charts and to use the glossary words where appropriate.

LMS CONNECTION

- The LMS may be modeling identification of quality products all year long as other classes display their projects in the LMC. You can design an evaluative activity each time there are displays so students will really look at them, learn from them, and be better prepared when they are doing this step.

STEP SIX: PRODUCT

NOVICE

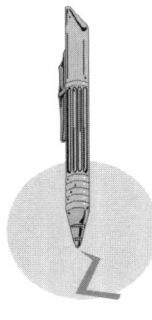

- If your children are non-readers or you are working on one product together, you may need to choose as a class which notefacts to include.

- Picture books work well for non-readers and writers. Students can describe their pictures during their presentation.

- An alphabet book illustrating key facts/words reinforces ABC skills.

ADVANCED

- Have a small group write songs, dances, a play, or a puppet show about the topic that can be performed by the whole class. Scenery, costumes, and/or puppets can be created by other members of the class.

- Allow students to make additional products at home. Be sure they have copies of the notefacts they will need to make the product. A copy of the quality product checklist would also be helpful.

- If students are doing some independent research on a subtopic as an extension activity, have them develop a product to share the information with their classmates.

MINI-LESSON
DEVELOPING A CHECKLIST FOR A QUALITY PRODUCT

Curriculum Unit: _____ *(Your Topic)*

Step 6: Product

Time: 45 minutes

OBJECTIVES
Students will
   Produce final edited documents and projects *(Key Skill 3)*.

MATERIALS
- Samples (enough for groups of two to four) of quality products like those you are making (posters, books, models, dioramas, etc.).
- Blank chart paper
- Markers

PROCEDURE

1. Explain to your students that:
   - At Step 6, researchers make something (a product) that shares their new knowledge with others.
   - This product needs to be of high quality.
   - They will develop a plan/checklist to help them make the best product.

2. If you haven't done so earlier in the unit, tell them what the product is, who the audience will be, and when the product will be presented to the audience.

3. Show them a quality sample of the product they will be making.

4. Ask them to identify one or two criteria (attributes) that make this a quality product, and write them on a piece of chart paper.

5. Now that you've modeled this for them, hand out quality samples to small groups of students and have them list as many criteria as they can that make the sample a quality product.

6. List the different criteria from each group on the chart paper, combining those that are similar.

7. Discuss what the most important criteria are, star them, and rewrite them on a new chart, leaving room under each one for indicators (details).

8. Be sure that "facts" is one criterion since the purpose of the product is to share new information about the class topic.

9. Next look at each criterion and ask your students to tell you some indicators about it that will help them make the best product. For example, a fact must be accurate information

10. List these indicators on the chart.

11. Have the students refer to this checklist as they make their products.

STEP SIX: PRODUCT

NOTES

- The product samples can be commercially made, samples from previous years, or pictures of quality products.

- Be sure you have identified the key attributes of the quality product before the lesson, but be willing to accept others that your students consider important.

- With a very young class, write only the main attributes and then talk about the details without writing them down.

- Be sure to teach the students the skills they need to make a quality product.

- If the students are making their products at home, give each one a copy of the checklist to use at home.

Figure 16:
Quality Products Checklist

STEP 6: PRODUCT IN ACTION

STEP 6: PRODUCT
MS. KACHINA'S 1ST GRADE HOPI UNIT

- Have students decorate class map with drawings and cutouts of symbols representing different notefacts categories to be used as a backdrop for mini-museum.

- Set up five centers where students will make artifacts for museum display:
    FOOD—Models of corn; grind corn and make piki bread.
    HOUSING—Build adobe homes from boxes and other art supplies.
    WEAVING—Baskets (women) and cloth (men).
    POTTERY—Clay pots.
    PICTURE DICTIONARY—Use words from glossary.

- Art teacher will work with students to make Kachina masks.

- Music and physical education teachers will work with students to learn hoop dance.

- Have students make invitations to the mini-museum day for parents and other classes in school. Include necessary information and Hopi symbols and art work.

It's time to put all the students' new knowledge to work for the mini-museum day.

First, Ms. Kachina works with the students to decorate the class map. Each child makes a cutout of a symbol to illustrate one notefact. Included are crops, pueblos, mesas, jewelry, pottery, baskets, kivas, fires, dances, masks, and dolls. When placed on the map, they make an informative and colorful backdrop for the museum. She hangs the organized notefacts next to it along with the Concept Map, Glossary, and Goal Setting charts. Agent IIM on the bulletin board completes the setting.

For the next five days, Ms. Kachina has parent volunteers help with the five workstations where the students prepare Hopi food, build models of pueblos, weave baskets and cloth, make clay pots, and create a picture dictionary of Hopi words. At each station, Ms. Kachina has hung the general checklist they have used for defining quality products. By the end of the week, each center is full of wonderful products representative of the categories from their notefacts. The children learn the hoop dance in music and P.E., and make Kachina masks in art. For language arts, they write and distribute invitations to their parents and the other 1st grade classes. Finally, everything is ready for the big day when they will showcase what they've learned.

STEP SIX: PRODUCT

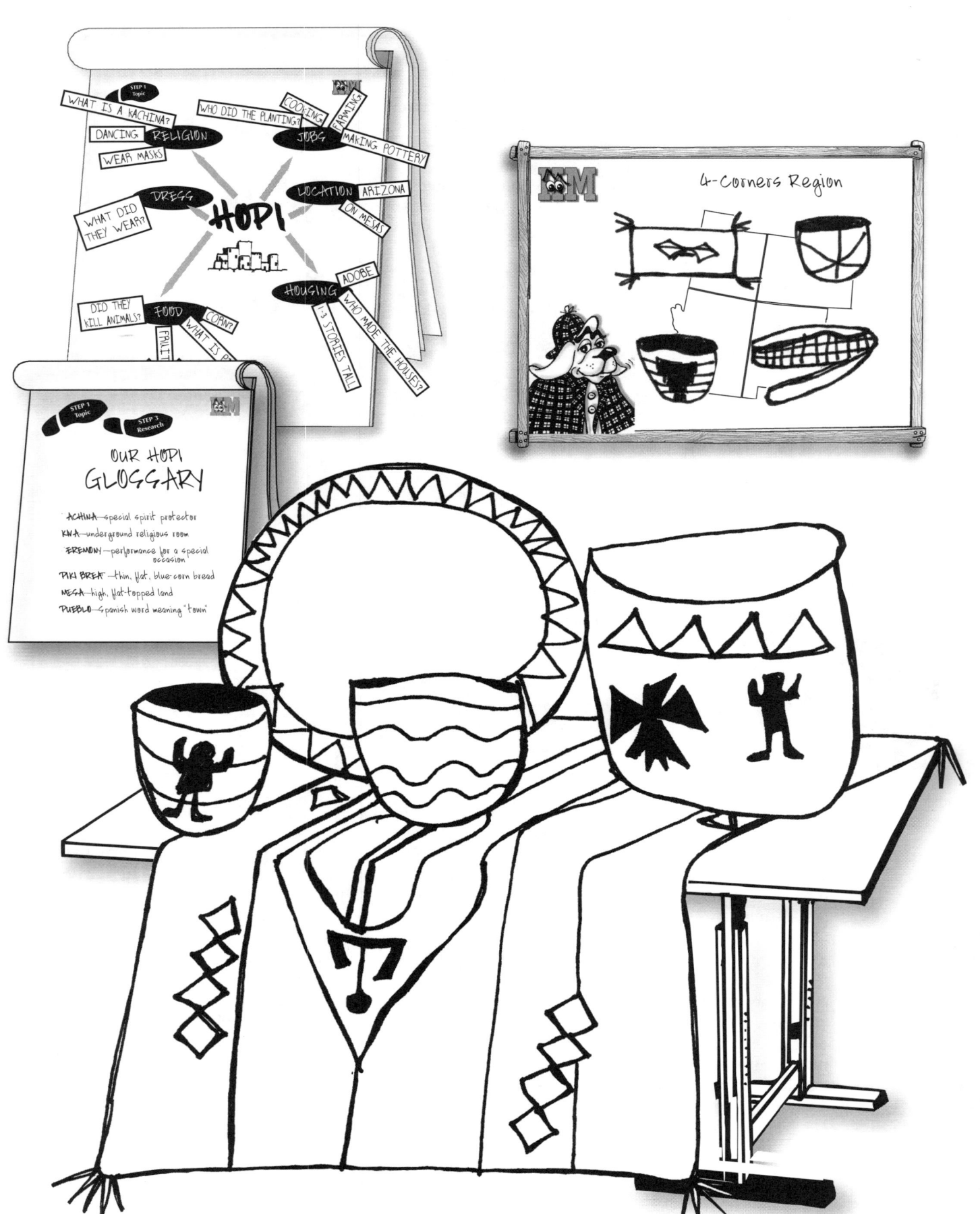

Figure 17:
Hopi Final Presentation

STEP SIX: PRODUCT

CHOOSING A PRODUCT

The purpose of any product is for students to show what they have learned during research. Your students have done a group study, but the product they make could be either a group or an individual one. Teachers have success with all types of products, but we have divided ours into categories that may guide you in making a selection that matches your students' grade and skill level.

GROUP PRODUCTS

By youngest students or first-time researchers

Bulletin board	Flannel board story	Quilt
Class book (ABC, fact, flip, picture, poetry, riddle, shape)	Game (board, vocabulary, memory)	Song—familiar tune with new words
Fact chart	Map	Treasure hunt

By older students or more experienced researchers

Advertisement	Mini-museum	PowerPoint presentation
Cartoon strip	Mural	Puppet show
Magazine	Newspaper	Timeline

INDIVIDUAL PRODUCTS

By youngest students or first-time researchers

Book (picture with facts, shape, with sentence starters)	Costume	Mobile
Clay model	Flag	Poster
Collage	Mask	Project cube

By older students or more experienced researchers

Book (biography, diary, fantasy, science fiction)	Hyperstudio presentation	Musical instrument
Demonstration	KidPix presentation	Puzzle
Diorama	Movie in a box	Travel brochure

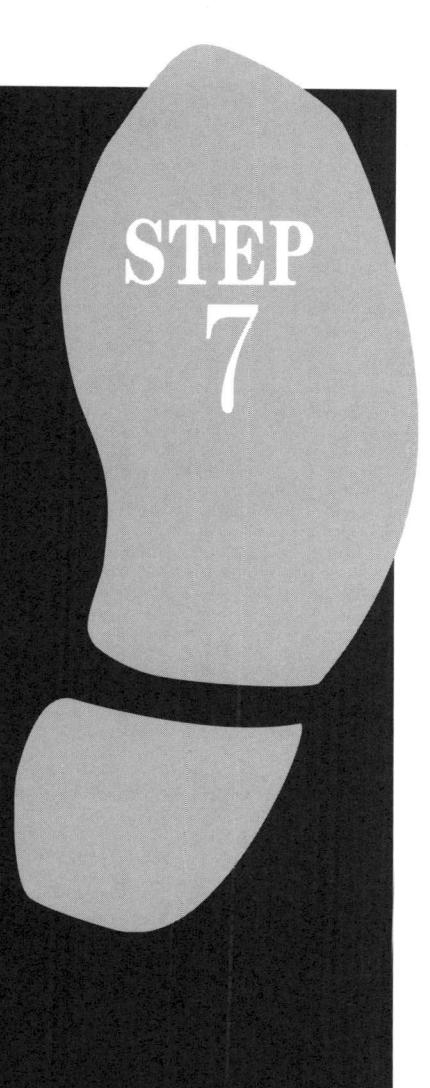

STEP 7

PRESENTATION

Your students will present their product(s) to an appropriate audience.

Introduction

The big day is approaching. Your students will present their new knowledge to an audience. If you matched the product your students have made to the audience that will receive it, everyone will feel satisfied. Teaching others about the class topic is extremely important. If there's a written component to your students' products, it's time to collect and evaluate them. However, presentations that will catch and hold their audience's attention need to be much more than the reading of reports.

The audience can be your students' classmates, another class, assembled parents, a newspaper editor, senior citizens, etc. Just be sure that the audience will be interested in the study's findings and the products your students have made.

Prepare for success on presentation day by helping your students hone their public-speaking skills. Model the key skills they need to use and leave enough class and at-home time for them to practice, practice, practice. This will build confidence and allow them to sound like the experts they have become.

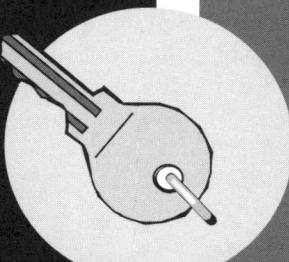

KEY SKILLS

The student will
1. Present information in various formats.

2. Use speaking strategies effectively.

3. Practice and use identified presentation skills: eye contact, voice tone, volume, pace, etc.

4. Speak appropriately to different audiences for different purposes and occasions.

STEP SEVEN: PRESENTION

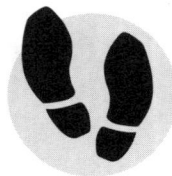
TEACHER STEPS
You will

a. Choose an appropriate audience for your students' product(s).

b. Identify the key public-speaking skills your students will need.

c. Explain to your students that they are now on Step 7: Presentation.

d. Work with your students to develop key skills for the presentation style you have chosen (mini-lesson, p. 58).

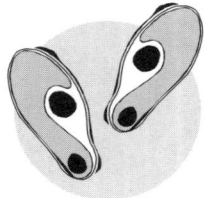
STUDENT STEPS
Your students will

a. Practice the targeted presentation skills.

b. Display those skills when presenting to the chosen audience.

c. Share information from the topic studied.

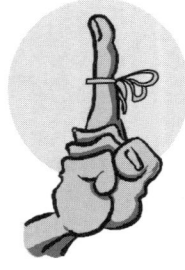
TEACHER TIPS

- Your students can be practicing their presentation skills throughout the unit. For example, have them read class texts out loud to their classmates and use a pointer during show and tell.

- Dedicate at least two class periods to formal practice for the final presentation. Practicing in class with presentation equipment (easel, pointer, microphone, etc.) helps students develop self-confidence and poise in front of an audience.

- You can send home presentation directions so students can practice with their families.

- Fact books your students write can be used in the library as resources for other classes. They could also do a reading in the library to another class.

- Audiences who would be interested in your topic might be a younger class, other classes at your grade level, or older reading-buddy classes.

- Inviting parents to the presentation is a wonderful way to share the experience with them.

- Unless they are reading pages of a book to an audience, the students should speak to the audience, not read a prepared paper.

- If your grade level has divided the main topic into sub-topics for each class, it is important that the children learn from each other in order to be knowledgeable about the main topic. Your audience will be the other classes, and your students will be the audience for the other classes' presentations.

- Work with your students on the skills necessary to be a quality audience.

LMS CONNECTION

- If space in your room is tight, consider working with the LMS to use media space. They may also provide good audiences if there are regularly scheduled classes.

- Practicing presentations in the media center allows for a different environment, a new adult, and some different feedback.

RESEARCH IN THE REAL CLASSROOM: The Independent Investigation Method for Primary Students

NOVICE

- Let your students present to small groups within the class if they are nervous about presenting to a large group.

- Sitting in a circle makes presentation time less intimidating.

- Puppets and costumes help shy children become more comfortable with speaking in front of an audience.

ADVANCED

- If individuals do independent studies as part of the class unit, they will need to practice the specific skills necessary to present their information and products to their classmates.

- Capable public speakers can be the MC's of your production.

STEP SEVEN: PRESENTION

MINI-LESSON
PRATICE IN PRONUCIATION, ENUNCIATION AND VOICE TONE QUALITY

Curriculum Unit: _____ *(Your Topic)*

Step 7: Presentation

Time: Several reading class periods

OBJECTIVES
Students will
> Use speaking strategies effectively *(Key Skill 2)*.
> Practice and use identified presentation skills: eye contact, voice tone, volume, pace, etc. *(Key Skill 3)*.

MATERIALS
- Reading texts
- Chair or raised platform

PROCEDURE

1. Explain to your students that in Step 7, researchers present what they have learned to an audience.

2. Find an interesting paragraph from a book you've been reading to your class, and present a short summary of it to them, speaking too quickly, mumbling, and using a soft and monotone voice tone.

3. Have a class discussion about why it was hard to listen to what you said and what things would make it easier to listen to someone.

4. Explain that for them to be good presenters, they will need to practice several of the things they mentioned: speaking slowly, saying each word clearly (enunciation), and using an enthusiastic voice loud enough to be heard.

5. Redo your presentation from the designated "presentation" chair or platform, making sure you speak slowly, clearly, enthusiastically, and in a loud voice.

6. Tell your students that they will practice during reading class this week by:
   - Finding an interesting paragraph in their reading book that they would like to explain to their classmates.
   - Standing on the designated chair (or raised platform) to show their classmates they are ready to present.
   - Waiting for you to ask "Are you ready?"
   - Explaining the main idea of their interesting paragraph, concentrating on speaking slowly, clearly, and in a loud, enthusiastic voice.

7. When each student is finished, ask the class these questions:
   - Was she excited?
   - Could you hear her?
   - Could you understand every word she said?
   - Can you tell me what her main idea was?

8. Using the class's answers, give a summary statement to the student, highlighting what was done well and what she needs to work on.

NOTES

- Be sure your students don't read their paragraphs.

- You might want to write the key skills on a chart as a reminder for your students as they are presenting.

- Another practice session could focus on different skills: introductory and concluding statements, eye contact, body position, etc.

STEP 7: PRESENTATION IN ACTION

STEP 7: PRESENTATION
MS. KACHINA'S 1ST GRADE HOPI UNIT

- Write and practice oral presentations about the Hopi culture, focusing on artifacts made in centers, map, hoop dance, and Kachina masks.

- As an introduction to mini-museum day, seven students will describe the steps of IIM.

- The other students will present information formally in "Speaker's Corner." These presentations will be scheduled every five minutes during the time the museum is open. An easel/poster will show time, speaker's name, and presentation topic. Parent volunteers will oversee this activity.

- The class will perform the hoop dance and serve piki bread to their guests.

- Ms. Jones will come in after mini-museum day to show Hopi Mesa slides as the culminating event.

The excitement is building. Four more days until the mini-museum opens its doors!

Invitations have been sent. The products are complete and displayed. The speeches for "Speaker's Corner" are written. The dance steps are learned, and the masks are ready to wear. The only thing left to do is practice speaking to an audience.

STEP SEVEN: PRESENTION

First Ms. Kachina reminds the students of what's on the quality presentation checklist: face and look at your audience; speak slowly and loudly enough to be heard; point to your artifact or IIM graphic; share facts about the topics; don't fidget. She then gives the students 10 minutes to practice in pairs, using the checklist for reminders. She walks around the room helping each pair.

Next, they practice in front of the class. They sit in their corners, waiting their turn, listening to their classmates. Ms. Kachina gently works with each child, telling him what he did well and what can be improved. The children then take their speeches and checklists with Ms. Kachina's comments home over the weekend to practice with their families.

Monday dawns, and the big day is finally here. The clock says 10:00 a.m., and the first guests arrive, ready to learn all about the Hopi and the Seven Step research process that helped these young children become researchers.

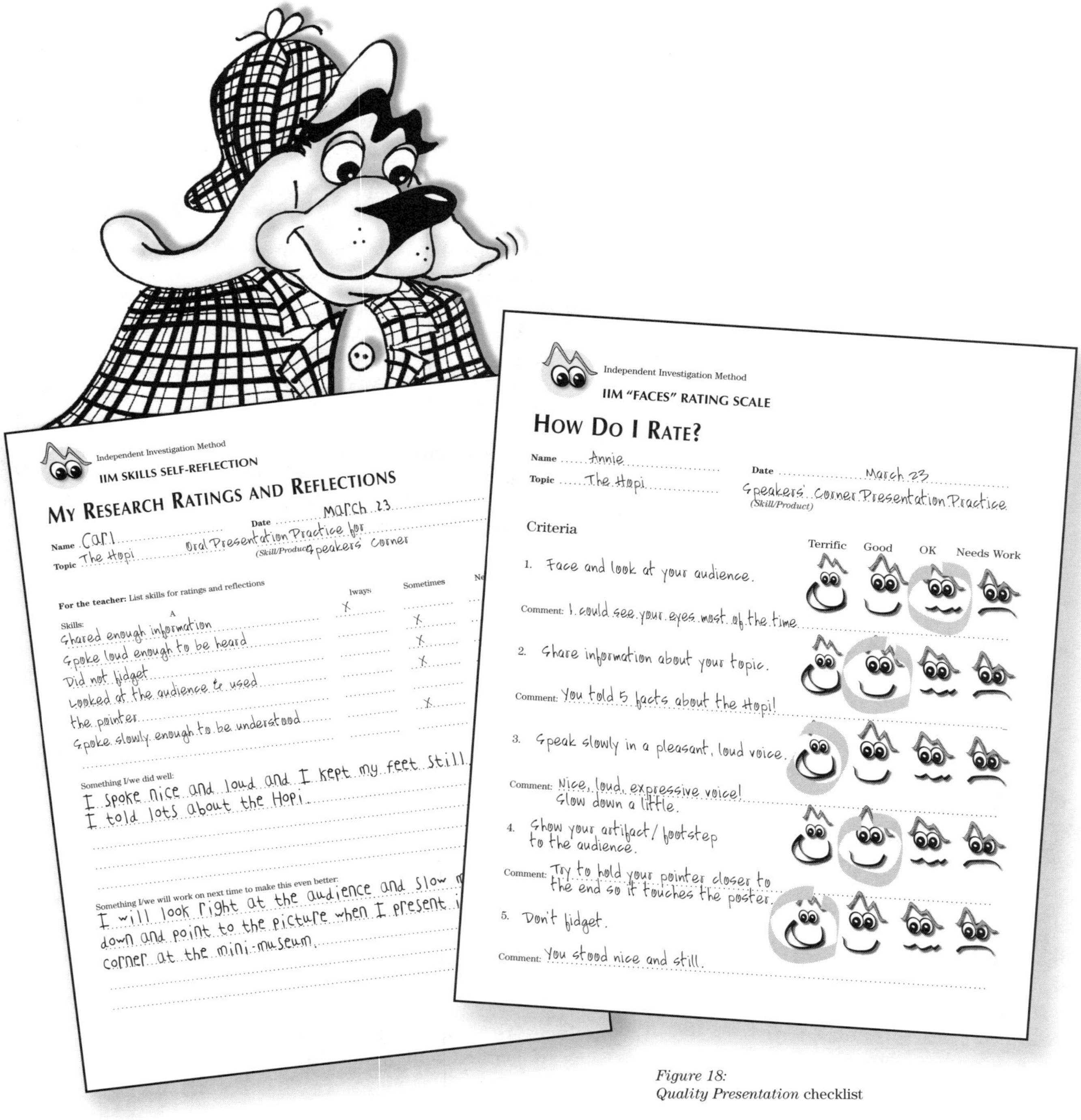

Figure 18:
Quality Presentation checklist

RESEARCH IN THE REAL CLASSROOM: The Independent Investigation Method for Primary Students

TEACHER RESOURCES

62 **IIM Unit Plan Forms**

74 **Assessment Forms**

90 **Sample MLA Citations for Various Resources**

92 **References**

UNIT PLAN: Independent Investigation Method

OBJECTIVES, SKILLS, AND STANDARDS

Curriculum Unit:

Whole Class Topic:

Time Frame:

Academic and Study Skills Objectives
Students will:

Teacher "Big" Questions
Write the broad, key questions that reflect the underlying purpose of the unit.

"How-to" Skills
Teach Students to:

Standards Addressed
What national, state, or local curriculum standards are being taught in this unit?

UNIT PLAN: Independent Investigation Method

OBJECTIVES, SKILLS, AND STANDARDS

Curriculum Unit: Native Americans of the Southwest

Whole Class Topic: Ms Kachina's class–Hopi Tribe

Time Frame: 4 weeks—1-2 class period(s) a day during reading and/or social studies

Academic and Study Skill Objectives
Students will:
1. Learn the 7 steps of IIM
2. Describe the physical environment of the Hopi including location, climate, landforms, and natural resources
3. Show ways the Hopi adapted to their environment
4. Understand how the Hopi have used ceremonies and stories to pass on their heritage and beliefs
5. Learn key vocabulary relating to the study of the Hopi
6. Develop questions to guide their research
7. Use multiple sources to locate information
8. Organize information in a systematic way

Teacher "Big" Questions
Write the broad, key questions that reflect the underlying purpose of the unit
- Why was the Hopi tribe able to survive in its environment?
- What are the roles/jobs of each tribe member?
- How do the Hopi pass on their traditions and beliefs?

"How-to" Skills
Teach students how to:
1. Identify directions (north, south, east, west) and state boundaries on an outline map
2. Write simple bibliographic headings for research sources
3. Use listening, observing, and questioning skills to gather new information
4. Record information without plagiarizing
5. Organize information in categories
6. Create invitations with necessary information and appropriate designs

Standards Addressed
What national, state, or local curriculum standards are being taught in this unit?
- Formulate questions and observations about familiar topics or new experiences
- Use multiple sources to locate information
- Organize information in systematic ways
- Represent and present information in a variety of ways
- Understand that cultures must adapt to their environment to survive
- Understand that cultures maintain their traditions and beliefs in different ways
- Know and locate cardinal directions and other major geographical features of the earth

IIM: TEACHER RESOURCES

UNIT PLAN: Independent Investigation Method

RESOURCES

Curriculum Unit:

Whole Class Topic:

Immersion Activities *(Ways to introduce the topic before research begins)*

Interest Center *(What you set up in your room to spark your students' interest)*

- Make IIM bulletin board with Agent IIM, the 7 steps, and the name of the research model, "Independent Investigation Method"
- Set up interest center—books, magazines, music, videos, artifacts, posters, . . . including strips with Big Questions
- **Possible resources for interest center or extension activities:**

Human Resources *(People to enhance and support unit activities)*

Resources for Step 3: Research *(Sources of information for the research portion of the study)*

Materials/Supplies *(Items you will need for all unit activities)*

UNIT PLAN: Independent Investigation Method

RESOURCES

Curriculum Unit: Native Americans of the Southwest

Whole Class Topic: Hopi Tribe

Immersion Activities *(Ways to introduce the topic before research begins)*
Read from *Myths and Legends of the Indians of the Southwest*. Santa Barbara, CA: Bellerophon Books, 1992.
Show *Native American Life*. American History for Children Video Series. Schlessinger Video Productions, 1996.
Play Hopi dance music: *Native American Indian Dances* (audio tape) by The Gray Eagles. Educational Record Center, Inc. 1-800-438-1637.

Interest Center *(What you set up in your room to spark your students' interest)*
- Make IIM bulletin board with Agent IIM, the 7 steps, and the name of the model, Independent Investigation Method
- Display books, magazines, music, videos, artifacts, posters, jewelry, corn, baskets, map
  . . . including strips with Big Questions
- Specific resources for interest center or extension activities

American Indian Songs (audio tape) by Dawley and McLaughlin. Music in Motion. 1-800-445-0649.
And It's Still That Way by Byrd Baylor. Santa Fe, NM: Trails West Publishing, 1976.
The Hopi by Elaine Landau. New York: Franklin Watts, 1994.
Native North American Stories by Robert Hall. New York: Thomson Learning, 1992.
The Pueblo Indians by Sonia Becker. New York: William Morrow and Company, 1985.
Native American Poster Set. The Paper Magic Group, Inc., Scranton, PA: 1997.

Human Resources *(People to enhance and support unit activities)*
Ms. Jones to show slides of trip to Hopi Mesas as culminating activity
Ms. Ball, phys. ed teacher, and Ms. Soprano, music teacher, to teach Hoop dance and music
Mr. Brush, art teacher, to make Kachina masks
Mr. Bookworm, library/media specialist, to help find resources, read Hopi legend to class, and work with advanced readers to gather additional notefacts
Parent volunteers to oversee center activities and speaker's corner

Resources for Step 3: Research *(Sources of information for the research portion of the study.)*
Source # 1: *The Hopi* by Elaine Landau. New York: Franklin Watts, 1994.
Source # 2: *Native Americans of the Southwest*. Videocassette. Educational Video Network, Inc. 1994.
Source # 3: Silver Moon—Hopi Native American Speaker

Materials/Supplies *(Items you will need for all unit activities)*
Chart paper, colored paper, glue sticks, markers, scissors, outline map of 4-Corners Region, colored butcher paper, 5x8 unlined index cards, clay, yarn, raffia, corn, bowls, hoops, boxes, poster paint, brushes, miscellaneous craft supplies

UNIT PLAN: Independent Investigation Method

ASSESSMENT

Curriculum Unit:

Whole Class Topic:

What process skills will you assess?   **How?**

What products will you assess?   **How?**

UNIT PLAN: Independent Investigation Method

ASSESSMENT

Curriculum Unit: Native Americans of the Southwest

Whole Class Topic: Hopi Tribe

What process skills will you assess?

1. Vocabulary development

2. Were goal setting questions answered?

3. Locate tribe using proper direction words on outline map

4. Organize information in a systematic way

5. Present to an audience

How?

1. Play vocabulary Jeopardy. Picture vocabulary cards. *IIM Glossary Chart (p. 15)*

2. Each student gives at least 1 fact relating to goal setting questions. *IIM Teacher Observation Checklist (p. 75)*

3. Mark Hopi location and direction compass on outline map of 4-Corners region. *IIM "Points" Evaluation (p. 79)*

4. Choose and defend category for notefact and place properly on chart *IIM Teacher Observation Checklist (p. 75)*.

5. Use in-class practice evaluation to work with family to improve presentation *IIM "Faces" Rating Scale (p. 87)* or *IIM Skills Self-Reflection (p. 89)*.

What products will you assess?

1. Symbols for class map

2. Written invitation to parents/classes

How?

1. Symbol accurately represents concept/item and is properly placed on map—*IIM Written Self-Evaluation (p. 81)* or *IIM 4-Criteria Rubric (p. 85)*.

2. All necessary information on invitation and artwork represents Hopi culture *IIM "Number" Rating Scale (p. 83)*.

UNIT PLAN: Independent Investigation Method

"PREP" STEP AND THE 7 STEPS

Curriculum Unit:

Whole Class Topic:

Briefly list what you will do to prepare for the unit and at each of the 7 steps of research.

"PREP" STEP

STEP 1: **Topic**

STEP 2: **Goal Setting**

STEP 3: **Research**

STEP 4: **Organizing**

STEP 5: **Goal Evaluation**

STEP 6: **Product**

STEP 7: **Presentation**

UNIT PLAN: Independent Investigation Method

"PREP" STEP AND THE 7 STEPS

Curriculum Unit: Native Americans of the Southwest

Whole Class Topic: Hopi Tribe

Briefly list what you will do to prepare for the unit and at each of the 7 steps of research.

"PREP" STEP

- Plan unit.
- Notify parents of upcoming unit and mini-museum day in class newsletter.
- Contact Silver Moon and Ms. Jones to schedule class visits.
- Meet with Ms. Ball, the physical education teacher, and Ms. Soprano, the music teacher, to discuss teaching Hoop dance and music.
- Meet with Mr. Brush, the art teacher, to plan lesson on making Kachina masks.
- Meet with Mr. Bookworm, the library/media specialist, to collaborate on resources, and on ways to reinforce the process and help advanced students.
- Contact parent volunteers to oversee center activities and speaker's corner.
- Set up interest center.
- Introduce IIM by dressing as a detective.

STEP 1: Topic

- Make *Concept Map* and *Glossary* chart.
- Mr. Bookworm reads Hopi legend to class.
- Show video of Hopi tribe as immersion activity.
- Identify location of Hopi on large map posted in interest center.
- Web information students know and questions they have about the Hopi on the *Concept Map* chart.
- Start *Glossary* chart with key words from immersion activities.

UNIT PLAN: Independent Investigation Method

"PREP" STEP AND THE 7 STEPS (continued)

STEP 2: Goal Setting

- Using question starters (who, what, where, when, why, and how), have students develop a list of questions about the Hopi related to our unit's Big Questions.

- Star six to eight questions that will be used along with the Big Questions to direct the class's research and write them on a *Goal Setting* chart to be displayed throughout the unit.

- Identify additional goals: using 3 resources, finding 35 notefacts, and learning 8 additional glossary words.

STEP 3: Research

- Prepare three *Notefacts* charts.

- Define plagiarism and notefact for students.

- Show *The Hopi*, and identify title and author.

- Write proper bibliographic information on *Notefacts* chart and "#1" in the magnifying glass to identify it as Source #1.

- Read the class a passage from the book, having them think of facts that relate to the goal-setting questions.

- Record notefacts on chart, putting a #1 in magnifying glass next to each notefact.

- Post *Notefacts* chart next to goal-setting questions.

- Do same steps with Source #2—*Native Americans of the Southwest* (video), and Source #3—speaker Silver Moon.

- Continue to add words to the *Glossary* chart.

- Mr. Bookworm works with top reading group to gather additional notefacts from the fourth source.

STEP 4: Organizing

- Prepare *Organizing Notefacts* charts with web categories on colored butcher paper.

- Read all notefacts with students, making sure they are complete and understandable.

- Have parent volunteers cut notefacts into strips.

- Model placement of notefacts on charts using several strips that can fit into different categories.

- Color handle of magnifying glass to match category choice, and glue on chart.

- Give remaining facts to pairs of students making sure there is a reader in each pair.

- Have students make decisions about category placement, explain choice and reasons to classmates, color magnifying glass handle, and glue notefact to chart.

STEP 5: **Goal Evaluation**

- Conduct an oral check to see if students have used three resources, found 35 notefacts, identified eight glossary words, and found answers to the goal-setting questions.

- Play vocabulary game to review glossary words.

- Have students fill out the My Words at Work form (p. 76) and make three picture and vocabulary cards illustrating and describing glossary words.

- Have students mark location of Hopi on an outline map of 4-Corners region and write at least one sentence describing where the tribe is located.

STEP 6: **Product**

- Have students decorate class map with drawings and cutouts of symbols representing different notefacts categories to be used as a backdrop for mini-museum.

- Set up five centers where students will make artifacts for museum display:
    FOOD—Models of corn; grind corn and make piki bread.
    HOUSING—Build adobe homes from boxes and other art supplies.
    WEAVING—Baskets (women) and cloth (men).
    POTTERY—Clay pots.
    PICTURE DICTIONARY—Use words from glossary.

- Art teacher will work with students to make Kachina masks.

- Music and physical education teachers will work with students to learn hoop dance.

- Have students make invitations to the mini-museum day for parents and other classes in school. Include necessary information and Hopi symbols and art work.

STEP 7: **Presentation**

- Write and practice oral presentations about the Hopi culture, focusing on artifacts made in centers, map, hoop dance, and Kachina masks.

- As an introduction to mini-museum day, seven students will describe the steps of IIM.

- The other students will present information formally in "Speaker's Corner." These presentations will be scheduled every five minutes during the time the museum is open. An easel/poster will show time, speaker's name, and presentation topic. Parent volunteers will oversee this activity.

- The class will perform the hoop dance and serve piki bread to their guests.

- Ms. Jones will come in after mini-museum day to show Hopi Mesa slides as culminating event.

UNIT PLAN: Independent Investigation Method

MINI-LESSON

Curriculum Unit: _____ *(Your Topic)*

    Step: _____

    Time: _____

    Lesson skill: _____

OBJECTIVES
Students will

MATERIALS

PROCEDURE

NOTES

UNIT PLAN: Independent Investigation Method

MINI-LESSON
NO MORE PLAGIARISM!

Curriculum Unit: Hopi Indians
Step 3: Research
Time: 10 minutes

OBJECTIVES
Students will

understand that researchers use many different types of resources to find information (Key Skill 1)

MATERIALS
- Chart stand and chart paper
- Interest center

PROCEDURE

1. Explain that in Step 3: Research, researchers use lots of "resources" to gather information about their topic.
2. Ask where researchers might find information about the Hopi.
3. Let them explore the interest center for ideas.
4. Make a list of their ideas on the chart.
5. Show them how many different resources they named.
6. Guide them to add others they haven't thought of: trip to Arizona, artifacts, posters, video, TV, speaker, museum, magazines, newspapers, food, poems, recipes, music, etc.
7. Star the resources they are going to use: a book, a video, and a speaker.
8. Introduce Source 1: The Hopi by Elaine Landau.
9. Continue with Steps B-1 (p. 25) to take notefacts from this resource.

NOTES

- We should add "resource" and "source" to our word banks.
- We could play a game to see how many resources we can think of. This could be part of our math lesson.

IIM: TEACHER RESOURCES

ASSESSMENT
IIM TEACHER OBSERVATION CHECKLIST

Topic _____

Step(s): _____

Ratings
YES   NO

BEHAVIORS OBSERVED

NAME OF STUDENT							COMMENTS

ASSESSMENT
IIM TEACHER OBSERVATION CHECKLIST

Topic: Hopi

Step(s): 4 & 5 - Organizing & Goal Evaluation

Ratings	
YES	NO

BEHAVIORS OBSERVED

NAME OF STUDENT	STEP 4 — Choose appropriate category for notefact	Give valid reason for choice	Place notefact in proper category	STEP 5 — Give at least 1 accurate fact			COMMENTS
Arnold	Yes	No	Yes	Yes			Couldn't give reason
Annie	Yes	Yes	Yes	Yes			Gave 3 facts
Carl	Yes	Yes	No	Yes			Mismatched color and category
Karen	No	Yes	Yes	Yes			Needed help with category
Mary	Yes	Yes	Yes	No			Gave inaccurate information
Paul	Yes	Yes	Yes	Yes			Good in all areas
Ralph	Yes	Yes	Yes	Yes			Good in all areas

IIM: TEACHER RESOURCES—assessment

Independent Investigation Method

GLOSSARY CHECK

MY WORDS AT WORK

Name .... **Date** ....

Topic ....

Write 3 words that are important to your study of ....
(Topic)

1. ....

2. ....

3. ....

Now, write 1 sentence using each word to show you understand its meaning.
Don't use just the definition.
Ex.   **No-No!** *A ball is a round toy.*
      Yes-Yes! *My friend was bouncing his rubber ball on the playground.*

1. ....

   ....

2. ....

   ....

3. ....

   ....

Independent Investigation Method

GLOSSARY CHECK

MY WORDS AT WORK

Name: Karen   Date: March 12

Topic: Hopi

Write 3 words that are important to your study of The Hopi
(Topic)

1. kiva
2. mesa
3. Anasazi

Now, write 1 sentence using each word to show you understand its meaning. Don't use just the definition.

Ex.   **No-No!** *A ball is a round toy.*
       Yes-Yes! *My friend was bouncing his rubber ball on the playground.*

1. The men climbed down the ladder to worship in the kiva.

2. The Hopi built their pueblos on three mesas called 1st mesa, 2nd mesa and 3rd mesa.

3. The Hopi learned about their ancestors, the Anasazi, by looking at their cave drawings.

IIM: TEACHER RESOURCES–assessment

Independent Investigation Method: "POINTS" EVALUATION

POWERFUL POINTS!

Name .... **Date** ....

Topic ....

....
(Skill/Product)

CRITERIA	POSSIBLE POINTS	MY POINTS
1.	....	....
2.	....	....
3.	....	....
4.	....	....
5.	....	....
6.	....	....
7.	....	....
8.	....	....
TOTAL	....	....

Comments: ....

....

....

Independent Investigation Method: "POINTS" EVALUATION

POWERFUL POINTS!

Name Paul **Date** March 13

Topic Hopi   Map of 4-Corners Region
(Skill/Product)

CRITERIA	POSSIBLE POINTS	MY POINTS
1. The map has your name on it.	5	5
2. The map has the 4 state names in correct place.	15	15
3. The map has a color key for the 4 states.	10	10
4. The map has each state colored according to the color key.	10	5
5. The map has an accurate direction compass.	15	15
6. The map is neat.	15	12
7. Your writing is legible.	15	15
8. Your spelling is correct.	15	12
TOTAL	100	89

Comments: This was very good work. Next time, check your spelling and work more slowly for neatness.

IIM: TEACHER RESOURCES – assessment

Independent Investigation Method

WRITTEN SELF-EVALUATION

LOOKING AT HOW I DID

Name .... Date ....

Topic ....
(Skill/Product)

I am happy about

....
....
....
....

Next time I will

....
....
....
....

One thing I learned was

....
....
....
....

I wish I could

....
....
....
....

Independent Investigation Method

WRITTEN SELF-EVALUATION

LOOKING AT HOW I DID

Name: Mary
Date: March 14
Topic: The Hopi
Map Symbol
(Skill/Product)

I am happy about how colorful my map symbol of the pueblo is.

Next time I will cut out the shape better.

One thing I learned was how to cut out the windows in the pueblo and put a picture behind them.

I wish I could make another map symbol. I would draw different kinds of corn.

IIM: TEACHER RESOURCES–assessment

Independent Investigation Method

"NUMBER" RATING SCALE

HOW HIGH CAN I GO?

Name .... **Date** ....

Topic ....
(Skill/Product)

CRITERIA	RATING	COMMENT

RATINGS

1 = Just beginning   **2** = Moving up   **3** = Made it   **4** = Over the top

Independent Investigation Method

"NUMBER" RATING SCALE

How High Can I Go?

Name Arnold
Date March 14
Topic The Hopi
Invitation to Mini-Museum Day Celebration
(Skill/Product)

CRITERIA	RATING	COMMENT
Accurate art work	3	Good detailed pueblo
Includes time, date, place	4	All information & details
Legible handwriting	2	Make letters larger
Proper grammar	4	All correct punctuation & cap. letters
Correct spelling	3	1 error
Creative	4	Wow! 3-D
Neat	2	Color inside the lines

RATINGS

1 = Just beginning **2** = Moving up **3** = Made it **4** = Over the top

IIM: TEACHER RESOURCES–assessment

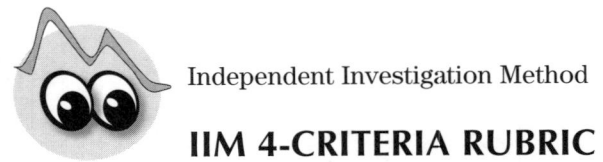

Independent Investigation Method

IIM 4-CRITERIA RUBRIC

1,2,3,4 - What is my Score?

Name .... **Date** ....

Topic ....
(Skill/Product)

For the teacher: List criteria for the skill/product and indicators for each rating number

Criterion:

1	2	3	4

Criterion:

1	2	3	4

Criterion:

1	2	3	4

Criterion:

1	2	3	4

Independent Investigation Method

IIM 4-CRITERIA RUBRIC

1,2,3,4 – What is my Score?

Name: Ralph
Date: March 16
Topic: The Hopi
(Skill/Product): Map Symbol

For the teacher: List criteria for the skill/product and indicators for each rating number

Criterion: Chooses Hopi item to represent as a map symbol

1	2	3 ✓	4
Not Native American	Native American but not Hopi	1 Hopi item in symbol	2 Hopi items in symbol

Criterion: Symbol accurately represents item

1	2 ✓	3	4
No relationship to item	Some accurate details	Accurate representation of items	Accurate, detailed representation of item

Criterion: Placement on Map

1	2 ✓	3	4
Far from correct area on map	Close to correct area on map	On correct area of map	On both correct area and landform

Criterion: Quality of Symbol

1	2	3 ✓	4
No quality indicators from #3 displayed	1 or 2 quality indicators from #3 displayed	Evidence of all quality indicators: colorful, neat, usable size	All quality indicators from #3 plus creative use of materials

IIM: TEACHER RESOURCES – assessment

Independent Investigation Method

IIM "FACES" RATING SCALE

How Do I Rate?

Name .... **Date** ....

Topic ....
(Skill/Product)

Criteria   Terrific   Good   OK   Needs Work

1. ....

Comment: ....

2. ....

Comment: ....

3. ....

Comment: ....

4. ....

Comment: ....

5. ....

Comment: ....

RESEARCH IN THE REAL CLASSROOM: The Independent Investigation Method for Primary Students

Independent Investigation Method

IIM "FACES" RATING SCALE

HOW DO I RATE?

Name ...... Annie .... Date .... March 23 ....
Topic ...... The Hopi .... Speakers' Corner Presentation Practice
(Skill/Product)

Criteria   Terrific   Good   OK   Needs Work

1. Face and look at your audience.

Comment: I could see your eyes most of the time.

2. Share information about your topic.

Comment: You told 5 facts about the Hopi!

3. Speak slowly in a pleasant, loud voice.

Comment: Nice, loud, expressive voice!
   Slow down a little.

4. Show your artifact/footstep to the audience.

Comment: Try to hold your pointer closer to the end so it touches the poster.

5. Don't fidget.

Comment: You stood nice and still.

IIM: TEACHER RESOURCES—assessment

Independent Investigation Method

IIM SKILLS SELF-REFLECTION

MY RESEARCH RATINGS AND REFLECTIONS

Name .... **Date** ....

Topic ....
(Skill/Product)

For the teacher: List skills for ratings and reflections

Skills:	Always	Sometimes	Never
....	....	....	....
....	....	....	....
....	....	....	....
....	....	....	....
....	....	....	....
....	....	....	....
....	....	....	....

Something I/we did well:

....
....
....
....
....

Something I/we will work on next time to make this even better:

....
....
....
....
....

Independent Investigation Method

IIM SKILLS SELF-REFLECTION

MY RESEARCH RATINGS AND REFLECTIONS

Name: Carl

Date: March 23

Topic: The Hopi

(Skill/Product): Oral Presentation Practice for Speakers' Corner

For the teacher: List skills for ratings and reflections

Skills:	Always	Sometimes	Never
Shared enough information	X		
Spoke loud enough to be heard		X	
Did not fidget		X	
Looked at the audience & used the pointer		X	
Spoke slowly enough to be understood		X	

Something I/we did well:

I spoke nice and loud and I kept my feet still. I told lots about the Hopi.

Something I/we will work on next time to make this even better:

I will look right at the audience and slow my words down and point to the picture when I present in Speakers' corner at the mini-museum.

IIM: TEACHER RESOURCES—assessment

Sample MLA Citations for Various Resources

Below is the MLA documentation style for each resource type. Especially at the Primary Level, you may choose to use an abbreviated version of this style on your Notefacts Headings.

PRINT SOURCES

BOOK: Author(s). *Title.* City of Publication: Publisher, Year.

Parker, Derek and Julia Barker. *Atlas of the Supernatural.* New York: Prentice Hall, 1990.

CHART, MAP, OR POSTER: *Title.* Map, Chart, or Poster. City of Publication: Publisher, Year.

The Solar System. Poster. Palo Alto: Dale Seymour Publications, 1997.

ENCYCLOPEDIA OR REFERENCE BOOK: Author (if given) or editor (name, ed.). "Title of article." *Title of Book or Publication.* Edition date (year only).

Pope, Clifford. "Crocodile." *Encyclopedia Americana.* 1994 ed.

MAGAZINE: Author(s). "Title of Article." *Title of Magazine.* Date: Page(s).

Satchell, Michael. "To Save the Sequoias." *U.S. News and World Report.* 7 Oct. 1996: 42-46.

NEWSPAPER: Author. "Title of Article." *Name of Newspaper* [City] Date, edition (if listed): Page(s).

Murphy, Sean. "It Floats." *Rockingham News* [Exeter] 21 May 1999, late ed.: A1+.

PAMPHLET: See Book.

NON-PRINT SOURCES

FIELD TRIP: Site. Location. Attending Group. Date.

Longfellow-Evangeline State Commemorative Area. St. Martinville, LA. Grade 6, Maplewood Middle School. 13 March 1997.

INTERVIEW: Person Interviewed. Type of Interview (personal, telephone, etc.). Date.

Parsons, Mary. Telephone interview. 30 May 1998.

SOUND RECORDING: Artist. *Title.* Medium (unless CD). Manufacturer, Year.

Kawamura, Masako. *Baratata-Batake.* Audiocassette. PWS Records, 1996.

SPEAKER:	Speaker. "Title." Sponsoring Organization. Location. Date.
	Landry, Bob. "Acadiens." Maplewood 6th Grade Team. Maplewood Middle School Auditorium. Sulphur, LA. 7 March 1997.
TELEVISION OR RADIO PROGRAM:	"Title of Episode or Segment." Performer, narrator, director, or author. *Title of Program*. Network. Call Letters, City. Date.
	"Secrets of Lost Empires." *Nova*. PBS. WGBH, Boston. 26 May 1998.
VIDEO:	*Title*. Director or Producer. Medium (unless film). Distributor, Year.
	Jurassic Park, The Lost World. Dir. Stephen Spielberg. Videocassette. Century Fox, 1995.

ELECTRONIC SOURCES

CD-ROM:	Author (if given). "Title of Section." *Title of Publication*. CD-ROM. edition, release, or version. City of Publication: Publisher, Year.
	"Whisky Rebellion." *Microsoft Encarta*. CD-ROM. 1996 ed. New York: Funk & Wagnalls, 1996.
INTERNET OR ONLINE POSTING:	Author. "Title." Online posting. Date of posting. Name of forum. Date of access <electronic address or URL>.
	Morse, Sarah. "Female Pedagogy." Online posting. 25 May 1997. Morse Homepage. 3 August 1998 <http://www.morsefamily.com>.

References

Armstrong, Thomas. *Multiple Intelligences in the Classroom: 2nd Edition.* Alexandria: ASCD, 2000.

Baum, Susan M., Sally M. Reis, and Lori R. Maxwell. *Nurturing the Gifts and Talents of Primary Grade Students.* Mansfield Center: Creative Learning Press, 1998.

Bromley, Karen D'Angelo and Judy Lynch. *Graphic Organizers.* New York: Scholastic, Inc., 1996.

Burke, Kay. *The Mindful School: How to Assess Authentic Learning.* Glenview: Pearson/Skylight, 1998.

Cassidy, Gail. "Curriculum for the Information Age." *Educational Horizons.* Fall, 1989: 42-45.

Eisenberg, Michael B, and Michael K. Brown. "Current Themes Regarding Library & Information Skills Information: Research Supporting & Research Lacking." *School Library Media Quarterly.* Winter, 1992: 103-110.

Eisenberg, M.B., and R.E. Berkowitz. *Teaching Information & Technology Skills: The Big 6.*

Gardner, Howard. *Multiple Intelligences: The Theory in Practice.* New York: BasicBooks, 1993.

Gibaldi, Joseph. *MLA Handbook for Writers of Research Papers.* New York: The Modern Language Association of America, 1999.

McKenzie, Jamie. *Beyond Technology: Questioning, Research and the Information Literate School.* Bellingham: FNO Press, 2000.

Starko, Alane J., and Gina D. Schack. *Looking for Data in All the Right Places.* Mansfield Center: Creative Learning Press, 1992.

Wray, David. "Teaching Information Literacy Skills in the U.K. Elementary Schools." *The Reading Teacher.* February, 1988: 520-524.

APPENDIX

94 **NCTE/IRA Standards for the English Language Arts**

96 **Definition of Terms Used in the Research Process**

99 **Reproducible Graphics**

NCTE/IRA Standards for the English Language Arts

The Research in the Real Classroom series is based on *Standards for the English Language Arts*, by the International Reading Association and the National Council of Teachers of English, copyright 1996 by the International Reading Association and the National Council of Teachers of English. Reprinted (below) with permission.

These standards are very broad and are applicable throughout grades K-12. Many states and individual school districts use them to form the basis of their mandatory skills assessments.

As we developed the Independent Investigation Method, we made sure that we grounded the entire process in these standards. Important learning outcomes—chosen from the standards and developed for the specific grade level of each core manual—form the focus of each step of IIM. We call these learning outcomes "Key Skills," and we list them at the beginning of each chapter that is devoted to a step of IIM.

Standard 1:
READING FOR PERSPECTIVE
Students read a wide range of print and non-print texts to build an understanding of texts, of themselves, and of the cultures of the United States and the world; to acquire new information; to respond to the needs and demands of society and the workplace; and for personal fulfillment. Among these texts are fiction and nonfiction, classic and contemporary works.

Standard 2:
UNDERSTANDING THE HUMAN EXPERIENCE
Students read a wide range of literature from many periods in many genres to build an understanding of the many dimensions (e.g., philosophical, ethical, aesthetic) of human experience.

Standard 3:
EVALUATION STRATEGIES
Students apply a wide range of strategies to comprehend, interpret, evaluate, and appreciate texts. They draw on their prior experience, their interactions with other readers and writers, their knowledge of word meaning and of other texts, their word identification strategies, and their understanding of textual features (e.g., sound-letter correspondence, sentence structure, context, graphics).

Standard 4:
COMMUNICATION SKILLS
Students adjust their use of spoken, written, and visual language (e.g., conventions, style, vocabulary) to communicate effectively with a variety of audiences and for different purposes.

Standard 5:
COMMUNICATION STRATEGIES
Students employ a wide range of strategies as they write and use different writing process elements appropriately to communicate with different audiences for a variety of purposes.

Standard 6:
APPLYING KNOWLEDGE

Students apply knowledge of language structure, language conventions (e.g., spelling and punctuation), media techniques, figurative language, and genre to create, critique, and discuss print and non-print texts.

Standard 7:
EVALUATING DATA

Students conduct research on issues and interests by generating ideas and questions, and by posing problems. They gather, evaluate, and synthesize data from a variety of sources (e.g., print and non-print texts, artifacts, people) to communicate their discoveries in ways that suit their purpose and audience.

Standard 8:
DEVELOPING RESEARCH SKILLS

Students use a variety of technological and information resources (e.g., libraries, databases, computer networks, video) to gather and synthesize information and to create and communicate knowledge.

Standard 9:
MULTICULTURAL UNDERSTANDING

Students develop an understanding of and respect for diversity in language use, patterns, and dialects across cultures, ethnic groups, geographic regions, and social roles.

Standard 10:
APPLYING NON-ENGLISH PERSPECTIVES

Students whose first language is not English make use of their first language to develop competency in the English language arts and to develop understanding of content across the curriculum.

Standard 11:
PARTICIPATING IN SOCIETY

Students participate as knowledgeable, reflective, creative, and critical members of a variety of literacy communities.

Standard 12:
APPLYING LANGUAGE SKILLS

Students use spoken, written, and visual language to accomplish their own purposes (e.g., for learning, enjoyment, persuasions, and the exchange of information.)

Definition of Terms Used in the Research Process

Analyze To identify the component parts of a whole.
Ex: Pueblo: stone, wooden beams, adobe mud, kiva . . .

Bibliography A record of all sources used for fact gathering in the research study using MLA format:
Ex.1: Book: Author(s). Title. City of publication: Publisher, Date.
Ex. 2: Video: Title. Director or producer. Medium (unless film). Distributor, Date.

Concept Map A web-like graphic organizer formed by collecting and organizing information.
Ex.:

Data Facts or figures from which conclusions or interpretations may be drawn.
Ex. Hopi - peaceful people; 3000 alive today; ancestors-Anasazi

Glossary: A list of specials or technical words with their definitions.
Ex. Kiva-an underground ceremonial chamber.

Goal Evaluation An accurate, measured appraisal of the goals set, data collected, the process used, and the skills developed during the research study.
Ex. Use five glossary words accurately in a paragraph about the Hopi

Fact Book Non-fiction books that are especially useful in research.
Ex. The Hopi by Elaine Landau

Graphic Organizer Any number of visual representations that organize information into categories or sequence.
Ex. Concept map, Venn diagram, timeline, outline . . .

Immersion Activities Ways to introduce a new unit and raise the class's interest and excitement.
Ex. Speaker, story, video, field trip . . .

Independent Study A research project where a student works independently to study an individual topic either of choice or one assigned by the teacher.
Ex. Class topic: Native American tribes - Independent Studies: Mary - Apache, Joe - Cherokee, Susie - Mohawk . . .

Interest Center A display of materials representative of the research unit topic that are chosen to raise the curiosity and interest of the students.
Ex. Books, magazines, pictures, posters, artifacts, models, newspaper articles, letters, clothing . . .

Key Skill The specific targeted skills taught at each step that are based on the NCTE/IRA Standards for the English Language Arts.
Ex. NCTE Standard 4: Students adjust their use of spoken, written and visual language to communicate effectively with...
Step 7–Key Skill: Speak appropriately to different audiences for different purposes.

KWL Chart A chart to organize research that is divided into three parts: K (what I already know), W (what I want to learn), and L (what I learned).
Ex. Topic: Hopi

K	W	L
Live in Arizona	*How do they get water?*	*Irrigate crops in valleys*

Materials/ Supplies The "things" needed for the specific unit being taught.
Ex. Chart paper, Glossary, Notefacts, and Organizing charts, markers . . .

Mini-Lesson Sample lessons used to teach the Key Skills at every step.
Ex. Step 1: Topic: How to make a class Concept Map chart (p. 13)

Notefact A short, true piece of information extracted from a variety of sources (book, video, field trip . . .) that the teacher records on chart paper (see Step 3: Research for a more complete explanation).
Ex. Hopi crops - corn, beans, squash

Objectives	The expected outcomes from the unit. *Ex. Students will learn the 7 steps of IIM, show ways the Hopi adapted to their environment . . .*
Paraphrase	Rephrasing the author's words and ideas without copying and without changing the intent of the author. *Ex. Direct quote: "Hopi agriculture includes raising corn, beans, and squash which the men . . ."* *Paraphrase: Hopi crops - corn, beans, squash*
Plagiarism	Copying someone else's words and/or ideas without giving him/her credit. *Ex. Hopi agriculture includes raising corn, beans, and squash which the men . . .*
Process Skill	Specific skill used in action learning. *Ex. Writing notefacts, categorizing notefacts, developing questions . . .*
Product	The paper or project that is created by the student to share research findings. *Ex. Book, play, poster, diorama, timeline, mural, song . . .*
Presentation	The way students share their product with others. *Ex. Reading a book they've written, acting in a play, speaking to another class . . .*

Questions	• Big Question - Broad, key question that reflects the underlying purpose of the unit
	  Ex. How did the Hopi adapt to their environment to survive?
	• Floodlight - Broad question
	  Ex. What kind of food did the Hopi eat?
	• Spotlight - Narrow, focused question
	  Ex. Who cooks the food?

Research	Focused investigation and experimentation about a topic to discover new facts. *Ex. Ms. Kachina's class set goals to learn many new facts about the Hopi Indians.*
Resource	Anything used to gather information for a research study. *Ex. Book, poster, interview, video, experiment, survey . . .*
Rubric	A scoring form used to evaluate process and product consisting of: Criteria - Component parts of any product/process to be rated. *Ex. Poster: Design Elements* Indicator - specific, objective detail to help rate criteria. *Ex. Poster design elements: colorful, neat, organized, creative*
Skill	A learned task needed to develop the minimum competencies referred to in the standards. *Ex. Organizing prior information on a concept map; writing notefacts . . .*
Source	The specific documented resource from which notefacts are written. *Ex. Source #1 - Landau, Elaine. The Hopi. Chicago: Children's Press, 1987.*
Standards	Minimum competencies on which to base grade level achievement at the national, state, or local level. *Ex. Gather, evaluate, and synthesize data from a variety of sources . . .*
Synthesize	To put research data together into a whole that expresses a new idea or creates a new product. *Ex. The first grade students in Ms. Kachina's class use the Hopi facts they gathered from three sources to create a play and cook Hopi food.*

Reproducible Graphics

IIM: APPENDIX

 INDEPENDENT INVESTIGATION METHOD

 INDEPENDENT INVESTIGATION METHOD

 INDEPENDENT INVESTIGATION METHOD

 INDEPENDENT INVESTIGATION METHOD

PREP STEP
Laying the Groundwork

STEP 1
The Topic

STEP 1
The Topic

PREP STEP
Laying the Groundwork

STEP 2
Goal Setting

STEP 3
Research

STEP 2 Goal Setting

STEP 3 Research

STEP 4
Organizing

STEP 5
Goal Evaluation

STEP 5
Goal Evaluation

STEP 4
Organizing

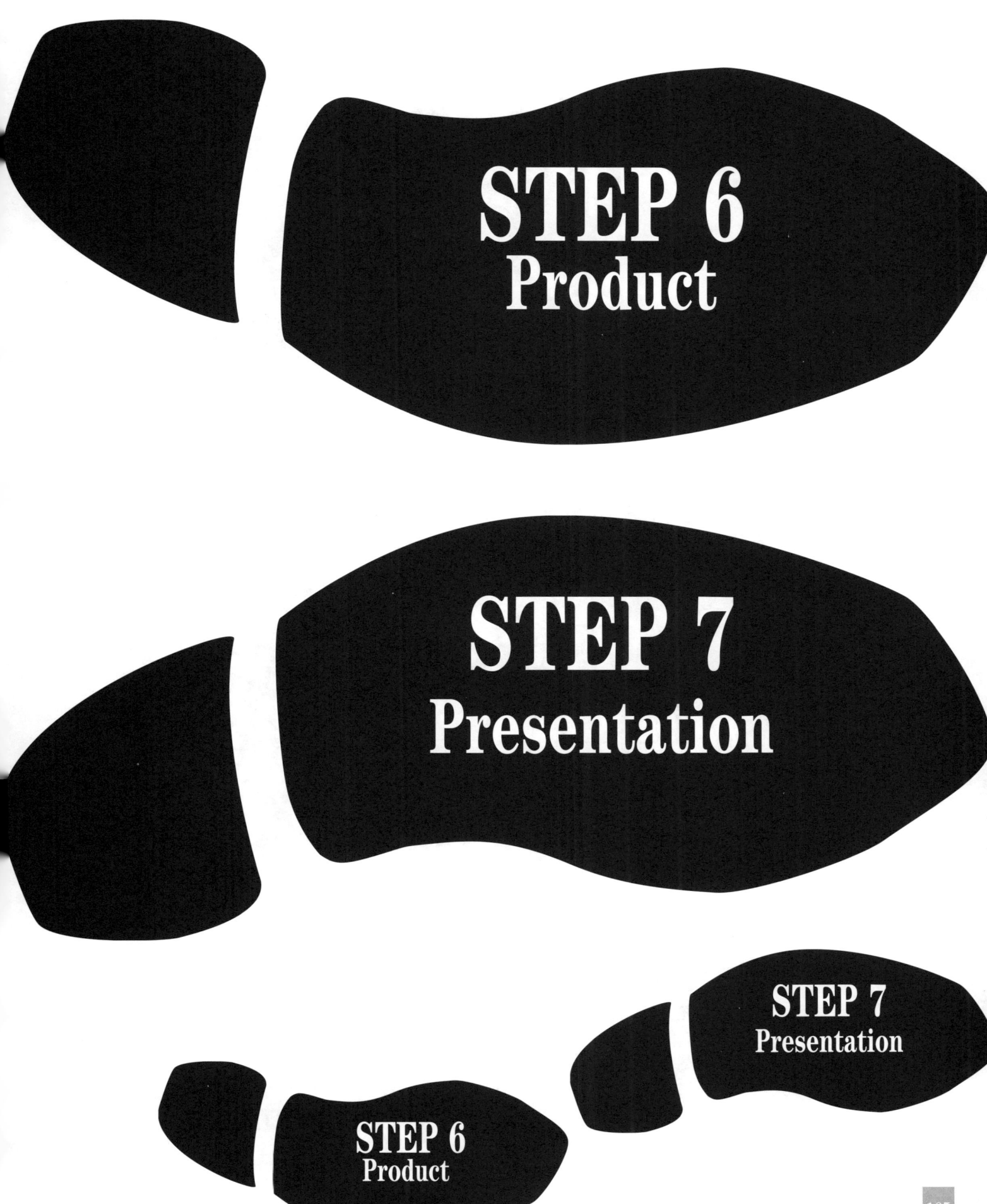

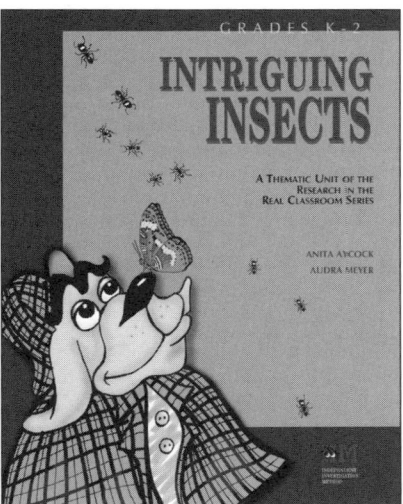
Insects (MH# 100)

Magnets (MH# 101)

Plants (MH# 102)

Presidents (MH# 103)

Rainforests (MH# 104)

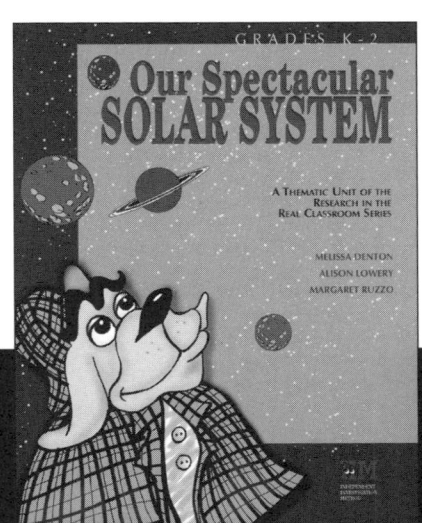
Solar Systems (MH# 105)

Discover IIM theme books

Now that you're familiar with *Research in the Real Classroom*, try these complete thematic units for the Primary Level. Lessons for each step of the IIM process are provided and made appropriate for every primary student. These new resources from Maupin House make getting started simple.

$13.95 each

800-524-0634
www.maupinhouse.com

Available Now
from Active Learning Systems

IIM Resources

These resources for you, your students, and their parents are the foundation of the IIM model.

IIM: Independent Investigation Method Teacher Manual (K-12) 2003 edition - $36.95
The Basic Level reproducible student workpages and IIM Assessment pages from the IIM Teacher Manual are written in Spanish to offer support to our Spanish-speaking students. Item Code: IIMTM

Spanish Version - IIM Student Workpages - $14.95
These double-sided Workpages give the English version on one side and the Spanish version on the other. Item Code: IIMSV

IIM CD - Companion to IIM Teacher Manual (1999, 2000, 2002 editions) - $29.95
Create and store units as well as customize and print all reproducible workpages and assessment forms. Item Code: 1999 - 2002 editions: IIMCD1 • 2003 edition: IIMCD2

IIM Teacher Manual and CD set - $59.95
Purchase both and save. Item Code: IIMS

Let's Research Native Americans - Primary: $13.95; Intermediate: $19.95
These thematic units teach the skills of the IIM research process as well as Native American history. The Primary book (K-3) presents a whole class research project about Eastern woodlands tribes; the Intermediate book offers both individual and cooperative group research studies on North American tribes. Across the Curriculum activities in language arts, math, science, and the arts make these complete studies.
Item Code: Primary -NAP • Intermediate - NAI

The Parent Guide to Raising Researchers: book and CD - $24.95
Based on IIM, this set will help parents get their children from "Oh, No!" to "Oh, Yes!" in research assignments. Hundreds of ideas and strategies on how to create a positive home atmosphere for research are supported by reproducible pages in the book and on the CD. Students ages 8 - 18 can do a complete research study on the reproducible forms or electronically using the CD. Item Code: PGRR

TEACHING TOOLS
Reinforce and enhance your students' research skills with these powerful tools.

Bulletin Board Set (Elementary) - $9.95
This lively set includes cutouts of the 7 footsteps, an IIM sign, and Agent IIM in his detective garb. Item Code: BBS

7 Steps to Successful Research (Poster) - $ 9.95
Keep your students focused on the steps of the IIM research process with this colorful, concise presentation of the 7 steps. Item Code: 7SSR

Just Say "No" to Plagiarism (Poster) - $9.95
Send a powerful message to your students: good researchers don't copy! Give them some tips on what to avoid. This poster does the job. Item Code: PP

Good Question Cubes - 10 pairs @ $9.95
Do your students have trouble asking good questions to direct their research? Start their study with fun by letting them toss these red and blue cubes to develop powerful questions. The critical thinking skills are built right in. Item Code: GQC

Muffle Mat - 1 @ $6.00/ Set of 10 @ $50.00
Muffle the sounds and enhance your students' use of the Good Question cubes with the ideas presented on this padded mat: Bloom's Taxonomy words and tips to prevent plagiarism get them thinking. Item Code: MM

RESEARCH REWARDS
Use these items to support and reward your students for great research results.

Special IIM Agent Pin - 1 @ $1.00 / Set of 10 @ $9.00
Have students pin on these colorful badges (2.25") to identify themselves as "Special IIM Agents" during research time. Item Code: SAP

"Rockin' Researcher" Sticker - Set of 50 @ $3.00
Reward great work with bright yellow "Rockin' Researcher" stickers. Item Code: RRS

IIM Pencil - Set of 10 @ $5.00
These neon pencils proclaim that "IIM researchers highlight key facts." They are available in neon pink, green, and yellow. Specify color for each set when ordering. Item Code: IIMP

IIM Highlighter - Set of 10 @ $9.00
"IIM researchers highlight key facts" in the color of their choice (yellow, pink, orange, blue, and green) Specify color for each set when ordering. Item Code: IIMH

Active Learning Systems

The Granary

P.O. Box 254, Epping, NH 03042

(800) 644-5059 • Fax (603) 679-2611

E-mail: info@activelearningsystems.com

Website www.activelearningsystems.com

If you liked
Research in the Real Classroom
The Independent Investigation Method for Primary Students
try these
other great teacher resources from **Maupin House**

Never Too Early to Write:
Adventures in the K-1 Writing Workshop. Bea Johnson

"Bea Johnson has hit a home run! Never Too Early to Write is very informative and motivating. 'Must' reading for everyone proclaiming to use developmentally appropriate and integrated language arts practices."
—Bob Kirschbaum, Elementary principal and national reading presenter o Spencer, IA

Improve reading readiness for kindergartners: start them writing! These ten effective writing-workshop strategies work in any literature-based setting or with any readiness series. A lovely and very useful resource.

Teaching the Youngest Writers: A Practical Guide.   Marcia S. Freeman

"...A well-written, valuable teaching resource, rich with classroom-tested models and writing techniques that emergent writers need."
—Brenda Parkes, Ph.D., author and literacy consultant

This classic and complete writing workshop resource takes your primary students from emergent to elaborative writers. Includes models for managing the writing process and explains the expository, descriptive and personal narrative writing techniques your students need to become fluent writers.

ISBN 0-929895-26-6, 143 pp. Index, Bibliography. Item #MH 42 • $19.95

2002 Doubleday Professional Book Club Selection

Primary Literacy Centers: Making Reading and Writing STICK!
Susan Nations and Mellissa Alonso

"With literacy demands higher than ever before, it is critical that we give students time to practice and apply the strategies we teach. Literacy centers provide authentic opportunities for students to practice and apply reading and writing strategies."
—Susan Nations & Mellissa Alonso

Standards-based literacy centers encourage the rest of the class to learn independently while you teach a small-group lesson. Connect reading and writing instruction with easy-to-maintain centers for Reading, Word Work, Listening, Research, Literature Response, Writing and Poetry. Your centers become focused places of learning where students apply, practice and master standards-based skills and strategies.

ISBN 0-929895-46-0, 208 pp. Index, Bibliography. Item #MH 78 • $23.95

Math, Manipulatives & Magic Wands:
Manipulatives, Literature Ideas, and Hands-on Activities for the K-5 Classroom
Karen Simmons & Cindy Guinn • Illustrated by Cindy Guinn

A little Bag Lady "magic" helps you integrate the language of math into every part of your elementary curriculum. Students learn national math standard skills through literature-based make-and-take projects. Helpful ideas, literature links and blackline masters make this a must-have resource that enriches the language-arts block and teaches the language of math to all students.

ISBN 0-929895-49-5, 192 pp. Bibliography. Item #MH 77 • $19.95

Maupin House

800-524-0634
www.maupinhouse.com